FAST FORWARD

WHAT IS YOUR COLLEGE DEGREE WORTH?

Tucker Matheson & Pichon Duplan

Cover design by Jared Matheson

Distributed by Amazon.com and (hardcopy publisher/ distributor)

ISBN: 1535225165
ISBN 13: 9781535225168
Library of Congress Control Number: 2016912123
CreateSpace Independent Publishing Platform
North Charleston, South Carolina

Contents

The Fast Forward Story

The inspiration to write Fast Forward was triggered by our observation that most college students do not have any idea of what they want to do with their lives after graduation, or how to figure it out. Working part-time as an adjunct professor for Suffolk University and as the cofounder of a leadership development nonprofit for students called iStandAbove, we experienced this trend through the students we taught and advised. We were also exposed to the flip side of the equation by seeing family and friends graduate college and enter careers completely unrelated to what they went to school for. Many of these same individuals were also heavily in debt due to student loans which held them back from chasing their passions and starting the life they wanted after college. It was obvious that some students were getting more value out of their college degree than others. We knew college was not a one size fits all experience, but we were aware of the intentional decisions we had made in college to both find a career path we were passionate about, and graduate in a good financial position. We wrote this book to give college students a playbook on how to maximize their return on investment in college and find careers they actually enjoy.

College is an amazing investment that many people in this world will never have the opportunity to partake in. Like any investment, college can either generate massive returns for you or set you back if not managed effectively. Use the tools and insight provided in this book to start crafting your own story of what your future will look like upon graduation. Mark Twain once said "The two most important days in your life are the day you are born and the day you find out why."[1] The time to take responsibility for your career is now, not after you graduate.

The fact that you have picked up this book means you are interested in maximizing your potential now, and not sometime in the future. Thank you for picking up our book and supporting not only us, but investing in yourself. Our mission is to inspire the next generation of young leaders to live out their passions and make a positive impact on the world. Help us spread the word by sharing what you learned with another student once you're done reading.

Enjoy the read and never stop the hustle!

CHAPTER 1

Maximizing Your Return On Investment

"It has been said that arguing against globalization
is like arguing against the laws of gravity."[2]
- KOFI ANNAN, SEVENTH SECRETARY
GENERAL OF THE UNITED NATIONS

Going to college and thinking about what you want to do for the rest of your life can be one of the most challenging and defining times in a person's life. We all go to college for different reasons, but the underlying motivation is the reward that lies at the end of it all: a degree. Why is a college degree so important? Statistics prove that higher education exponentially increases someone's career earnings and future prospects. Students with a four year college degree earn 74% more during their lifetime than those with just a high school diploma.[3] However, the ultimate value of a degree is directly dependent on two factors – (1) how applicable your degree is to your career goals and (2) how much you paid for it.

The first factor is translating what you studied in college to your career. Your criminal justice degree, will inherently be worth less if you later pursue an accounting career, than if you had graduated with an accounting or finance degree in the first place. This is because the skills learned are directly transferable to your job. It is important to note that many people graduate with degrees that are unrelated to their future career and go on to be very successful. However, this normally occurs only after they have spent a good portion of their time after college switching careers or pursuing further education in search of a career that motivates them. The point is that if you can match what you actually studied in college to your career, you are already ahead of the curve and your investment can be put to work immediately, therefore maximizing your return on investment.

The second factor that determines your return on investment in college is how much you paid for your degree and what amount of student loans you had to take on. The more you pay for college and the more debt you have, the less return on investment you can make on your degree. In order to start making a positive return on your education, you have to first pay back all your debt. This is easier to do if you can find ways to pay less for college, minimize your debt, and manage your expenses while in school. As we will learn, this starts by taking ownership of your finances right from freshman year.

What is your college degree going to be worth?

Today, students are faced with more pressure than ever before. Mounting education costs, rapidly expanding career options, and increased global competition for internships and entry level positions are forcing students to rush into "getting any job," as opposed to searching for careers that light a fire within them.

The answer used to be that having a college degree was enough to differentiate yourself, but that has changed over time. About fifty years ago, the number of individuals in the United States workforce who had some form of a college degree was only 28%. Fast forward to today, college is now the recommended path for approximately 66% of students coming out of high school.[4] This percentage will only continue to grow as the number of college students around the world is set to double to 262 million by 2025.[5] You are no longer competing against the students in your college, or even in your country. You are competing against students from all over the world for your dream career.

Globalization has become a buzzword that describes how the world is becoming drastically more connected than it was in the past. Human societies across the globe have progressively established closer contact over many centuries, but recently the pace has dramatically increased.[6] Technology has been a key enabler and is changing how governments and businesses interact, as well as how easily societies can access information and connect with each other. Think for a minute about how much technology has evolved during our lifetime. In the year 2000, much of the world did not have internet. Facetime, Google, and Facebook did not exist. Now, thanks to computers and smartphones, our access to people and new information is easier than ever. Jet airplanes, huge oceangoing vessels, and other sophisticated transport have enabled the rapid expansion of global trade. You can now order a product from your smartphone in London and have it gift wrapped and overnighted to you from China. These trends have made the world more interdependent than ever before while also increasing the rate at which the world operates.[7] Companies, organizations, and government agencies around the world have been forced to reevaluate how they operate globally. Due to globalization and innovations in technology, the types of careers that existed when our parents were ready to enter the workforce are greatly different from the careers of today.

The effects of globalization are putting more emphasis on how students are differentiating themselves from their peers in and outside of the classroom. Yet, many students do not know where to start. Most students graduate college either trying to get the first job that comes their way to gain experience, following a career path recommended by family or friends, or chasing the financial incentive of certain lucrative careers. Instead, the focus should be on finding careers that they are truly passionate about.

Careers that excite us encourage us to do our best work and make the biggest impact. It is hard to compete against a global talent pool of college students and young professionals when you are not doing something you enjoy. The way to get ahead is to dedicate the time to work on developing your skills and knowledge. Working in a career that thrills you will make dedicating additional time (e.g., late nights, weekends, and holidays) easier to do. Finding a career you are interested in allows you to outwork the competition and position yourself to accomplish things you never thought were possible. Take a minute to think about projects or activities you have done in the past that you enjoyed. Did you work harder? Did you work long hours and not think twice about it? When we are passionate about something, we care about the results and want to showcase our best work.

Stop for a second and think about the things you enjoy doing the most. What makes you smile when you wake up in the morning? Now go a step further and think about the experiences that have motivated you to take action. What gives you that push when everything else in your life is telling you to stop? Pause and think about these questions, and take the time now to reflect on what truly matters to you. If you read biographies of "successful" people, many times, they have values that guide them. Aligning what you enjoy doing with your values and motivations is one tried and tested way to feel fulfilled in your work.

As mentioned before, finding a career you are passionate about is only one important aspect of maximizing your return on investment. Students also need to ensure they are proactively managing their personal finances wisely to minimize education related debt. Students may not pay particular attention to their loans while in college, but find out quickly that they need to start making payments on their outstanding debt after graduating. Debt repayment can put pressure on recent grads, and in some cases, cause students to forego certain career and life aspirations such as renting an apartment or buying a car. Many students even have to move back in with their parents after college to save some money. By managing your finances throughout college, you can ensure that you can hit the ground running in your career after graduation.

In the chapters that follow, you will learn about three simple concepts that you can use to find which careers you enjoy most. These three concepts are: (1) Drawing on a blank sheet of paper, (2) Making connections, and (3) Creating your story. To bring the concepts to life, we interviewed several individuals who have created careers around their passions. These individuals were people we knew of through personal relationships or read about as being game changers in their respective fields in the United States. Their stories do not encompass all industries and careers, but they do showcase the principles of what it takes to make your vision of success a reality. To complement the three concepts and ensure you can fully maximize your college investment, we will also highlight how you can manage your personal finances to stay in control of your future after graduation.

Steve Jobs once proclaimed,

Your work is going to fill a large part of your life, and the only way to be truly satisfied is to do what you believe is great work. And the only way to do great work is to love what you do. If you haven't found it yet, keep looking. Don't settle. As with all matters of the heart, you'll know when you find it. And, like any great relationship, it just gets better and better as the years roll on. So keep looking until you find it. Don't settle.[8]

It is up to you to drive your own interests, design your pathway to success, and create the impact you want for yourself and your community. Why are you going to college? Even if you think your ultimate goal is to make money, what is the underlying motivation? Thinking about these questions is just the beginning of the process, but it is important that you get a head start on defining and securing your future. Use the core concepts outlined in this book as your roadmap for jumpstarting your career and maximizing your college investment. You are a small fish in a big pond, but you can be the first one everyone sees.

CHAPTER 2

Drawing On A Blank Sheet Of Paper

Some people will know exactly what they want to do at a very young age, but the odds are low. I feel like people in their early to mid-20s are very earnest. They're very serious, and they want to feel like they've accomplished a lot at a very young age rather than just trying to figure stuff out. So I try to push them toward a more experimental attitude.[9]

- STEWART BUTTERFIELD,
COFOUNDER OF FLICKR AND CHIEF EXECUTIVE OF SLACK

To start your career in college, change your mindset and take an exploratory approach. Life moves fast after graduation, so you want to be sure you are on the right path early on. That is why it is vital to experience your interests in college so that you can identify which careers you truly like and, more importantly, dislike. Every great painting or drawing once started out as a blank sheet of paper. Drawing on a blank sheet of paper in college means using your time to explore careers you are interested in firsthand, by actually trying them out. You can then pick out your likes and dislikes from each experience and make more informed career decisions going forward.

Most students make career decisions based on their perceived talents, preferences, and perceptions of certain jobs. For instance, being good at numbers and math automatically equates to majoring in accounting, finance, or engineering. Or being adventurous and a good writer means you would like journalism. At times, pressure from family, friends, and your community also contributes to determining your field of interest. These thoughts and influences often determine careers when they should only be the starting point, a hypothesis you approve or disapprove after experimenting with different activities and experiences first hand. The only way to truly find your passion is in practice, not in theory. By taking an exploratory approach to college, you can discover the true possibilities of what is out there. Developing an experimental mindset enables you to use the process of elimination to zero in on a career you will truly enjoy. Why wait until your junior year internship to find out you don't like the type of career you thought you wanted? The earlier you start trying out different types of careers, the better your chances are of finding the right career for you.

How can you start experimenting with careers that interest you?

(1) Reflect on Your Talents:
This is usually the end step for most students in determining their careers. Instead, use this step as a starting point to pinpoint certain

skills, interests, and talents that you think you enjoy. You will most likely think of more than one option. Spend time on the internet, watch videos, read articles, and reflect on what you think you are interested in. Take your blank sheet of paper and write down the things that excite you (e.g., acting, finding the cure for a life threatening disease, inventing the latest new product, etc.). The more specific you can be, the better. This will give you a good foundation to begin experimenting with careers that could potentially fuel your passion.

(2) Research Fields of Interest:

Once you have some fields in mind, begin researching different careers within that field. There is so much information at your disposal. Knowing your interests and most enjoyable skills allows you to begin matching them with professions and industries.[10] What careers and types of companies exist in those professions and industries? Talk to people who you see are ecstatic about their jobs. Ask yourself – could I do that, or is that not for me? Take notes, whether it's on your blank sheet of paper, your computer, or your smartphone. Keep track of these ideas. This research and insight will allow you to make informed decisions on which careers to pursue further.

(3) Map Out a Plan of Action:

Once you have identified a few careers of interest, grab that blank sheet of paper and map out at least two plans of action. How can you experience what that career is like in and outside of the classroom? You do not want to put all of your eggs in one basket. Maybe digital marketing is of interest to you, but you also want to learn more about international law. An example of two small experiments would be to try to find an internship or part-time job doing digital marketing and joining the law club or a similar organization at school. You are exploring both careers, but in diverse ways based on your level of interest at the time.

(4) Put It Into Action:

After you have your plan, it is time to put it into action. Apply for internship opportunities at digital marketing companies in your area. Find out what clubs and organizations the law school has and join them. The key is to get out of your comfort zone, put yourself out there, and take action. Many people hang on to action plans and do not execute on them because they fear failure. The young leaders of today understand that they are going to fail at some point and that it is a necessary part of growth and personal development. No one is perfect. The important concept is to always fail forward and use failure as an opportunity to learn and improve.

(5) Zero In On Your Career:

After repeating the concepts above and trying a variety of activities you are interested in, you can zero in on careers you enjoy the most. Developing new ideas, dropping uninteresting activities, elaborating on experiments to further pursue the interesting ones, and keeping an open mind are all part of the experience. By constantly evaluating which experiences you enjoyed the most, you can start zeroing in on the one or two careers that intrigue you the most.

Many students approach college thinking they need to figure out the big picture based only on what they are learning in the classroom. Thinking about the big picture of our futures and what we want to do upon graduation is a daunting task. The concept of drawing on a blank sheet of paper allows you to take small steps to overcome this uncertainty. Social scientists have argued that quick wins and gaining momentum are the most effective ways to tackle big problems.[11] Thinking of change and the future as something that requires massive steps forward creates fear and paralysis. Each additional attempt at trying something new gives you the opportunity to reflect back on what you did and did not enjoy. You can then refine, refocus, and zero in on specific interests that you are most passionate about. Learning as you go and constantly adjusting puts you in the best position to graduate college knowing that you are going down the right path.

It is important to note that finding a career that motivates and excites you is not something that happens overnight.[12] As you start experimenting with different careers, your heart will become your barometer. You will know when you find a career that lights a fire within you and you will also know when you absolutely hate doing something. Keep in mind, as you go through life, what you are passionate about may change. However, all successful people know their interests and motivations at any given time, allowing them to ensure they are making intentional decisions that align with their vision. Don't go through the motions in college thinking that you can figure life out later. The bus will have left the station by then and you will be running to catch it.

The next section of this chapter will introduce you to four of the eleven individuals we interviewed who have found careers that both excite and motivate them. These stories give you behind-the-scenes access into what these individuals did to draw on a blank sheet of paper. In addition, at the end of each story, we asked each interviewee to answer one question: If you could go back in time and tell the eighteen-year-old version of yourself one piece of advice, what would it be? Learn from their stories and advice and think about how you are going to maximize your time in college to start your own rewarding career.

—∿—

Stephanie Weiner
Investor, Bain Capital Ventures

Stephanie Weiner, a successful investor for Bain Capital Ventures, started drawing on a blank sheet of paper from a very young age. Growing up, Stephanie was involved in everything she possibly could be. At age nineteen, while in college, Stephanie was already serving as a founding member of Dorm Room Fund at the University of Pennsylvania. She also founded an ecommerce site in middle school, and attempted to launch several other start-ups in high school and college. She was the youngest investor to get named in 2015 to *Forbes'* "30 Under 30 in Venture Capital."[13] At twenty-two years old, Stephanie had already accomplished a tremendous amount and had found a career she was passionate about after graduation. However, what you don't hear about is all the hard work Stephanie had been putting in for years prior to make her post-grad career a reality.

Stephanie unknowingly had a knack for entrepreneurship even from childhood. At the age of six, she worked with her friends to put up a water balloon stand at the neighborhood beach in Long Island, New York. At the end of the day, the money earned was divided up and used to buy ice cream for everyone. Middle school was no different, as she made jewelry and even created a website as her platform for sales.

During her sophomore year of high school, Stephanie started an environmental club, "Help Our Planet Earth," or HOPE, to instill more emphasis on the importance of taking care of the environment. Under her leadership, HOPE flourished, growing to the point where it was divided into the recycling, gardening, public relations, and education branches. After a few months, about 120 students gathered for club meetings every Thursday, driven by an urge to help the environment.

Stephanie was driven to do everything possible to get into the school of her dreams, the Wharton School at the University of Pennsylvania (Penn). She was the founder of HOPE, an Intel Science Talent Search semifinalist, captain of the varsity tennis team, played varsity golf, and was a Chapter President for the Future Business Leaders of America. In accordance with her entrepreneurial spirit, Stephanie was also awarded fourth place nationally and first place in the state of New York in the Introduction to Business Competition. Not only was she exploring her interests outside of the classroom, but she was also maintaining an A+ grade point average. Needless to say, she got into her dream college through her hard work and dedication.

Transitioning from high school to college paved the way for a new mindset, as Stephanie began to focus on quality as opposed to quantity. She thought her professional goal was to one day run her own environmentally-focused nonprofit, so she planned to major in Environmental Policy. At the time, all of her peers were interested in pursuing careers in investment banking and finance. Stephanie heard these jobs paid well but didn't understand the infatuation her peers had with them.

Once Stephanie got settled into her first semester she decided to join the Entrepreneurship club and the Eco Rep club (focused on the environment). The Entrepreneurship club was part of the Engineering school and was set up like a technology start-up incubator. This was her first exposure to technology start-ups which would later become a core piece of her job at Bain Capital

Ventures. During her first semester, Stephanie was also offered an opportunity to work under an entrepreneur at Wishberry, a crowdfunding start-up. By getting hands on experience outside of the classroom, she confirmed her interest in technology and start-ups. To Stephanie, freshman year was for experimenting by trying out different activities that interested her before going in depth in any field.

During her sophomore year at Penn, Stephanie saw another opportunity come to fruition. The difficulty in finding sublets to rent her housing space while studying abroad in Australia led her to build a website with a friend that would solve this problem. The website was formed under the company, PennLets, where an online platform was developed with over 1,000 active listings for the subletting and leasing of off-campus university housing. Stephanie and her team created a marketing strategy and established relationships with local real estate market stakeholders in their effort to mitigate the housing challenges they faced before going abroad. The site is now a full-time service within the school and a permanent feature of the University of Pennsylvania's student newspaper, *The Daily Pennsylvanian*.

Although Stephanie was confirming her interest in technology start-ups, she was still curious about the finance industry. To appease her inquisitive mind, she attempted to secure a finance internship before she was scheduled to study abroad in Australia during her junior year. In her quest to secure a finance internship, she spent the entire winter break of her sophomore year studying and preparing. She traveled to and from New York City for interviews and ended up receiving an offer from The Blackstone Group, a financial services company. Fortunately, the duration of the internship was only six weeks, which fit perfectly into her schedule so as not to conflict with her plans to study abroad. She was assigned to a position within Blackstone's Private Equity group which was very uncommon for a nineteen-year-old. She worked with a team that helped companies identify ways to improve their operations. Stephanie enjoyed her experience at Blackstone, learned a tremendous amount, and gained hands-on experience.

Immediately after interning at Blackstone, Stephanie embarked on her study abroad program in Australia which allowed her to step away from the pressures facing a college student approaching graduation. She used this time to explore many activities she normally would not have, such as taking an art class, trying jewelry design, and backpacking to a number of interesting towns and cities. One day while abroad, Stephanie and her friends befriended a diving instructor from Germany who taught them the importance of finding careers you are passionate about in order to live a fulfilled and happy life. This encouraged Stephanie to further reflect on her past experiences and think about what she enjoyed and what motivated her the most.

While zeroing in on her passions in Australia, First Round Capital, a venture capital firm, sent an email out about an opportunity called the Dorm Room Fund to be started on Penn's campus. The Dorm Room Fund was an initiative designed to give students money to invest in projects of their choosing. This presented an opportunity to combine several of Stephanie's interests in venture capital, technology, and entrepreneurship. The opportunity would allow her to manage $20,000 a year in grants, giving out $1,000 at a time to students looking to start their own businesses. Stephanie described the First Round Capital opportunity as, "So exciting and really at the intersection of everything I liked!" However, Stephanie was in a bind about how she would get them to notice her from across the globe. She thought long and hard, and came up with a stellar way to introduce herself, her experiences, and why she would be a great fit for the role, by using the logos of First Round Capital's portfolio companies in her application.

Hi! My name is Steph.

It looks like you are about to StumbleUpon another application, but before you GroupMe with the others and throw this back into your TalentBin, I want to zoomin on why I think I would be an UBER addition to The Dorm Room Fund.

First, I am going to about who I am so that you can get to know me. I have a of interests including exploring nature, playing tennis, and just relaxing with my friends. I love to EAT Reese's Pieces, and I am as tall as a jirafe . Just kidding. I am Accptly into 5 feet.

While my motherknows why I'd be an awesome addition to 's Dorm Room Fund, I am going to Rewind a bit and SAY why I think I would be your . I'm an Upstart junior in the Wharton school. Satisfaction when I information about what's poppin in on-campus tech by hanging out at Weiss Tech House, working on a CustomMade app during PennApps, and Relaying my FLURRY of business knowledge during the Wharton Business Plan Competition. I myself about start-ups and investing when I worked for Wishberry, The Blackstone Group Private Equity, and my own Fab. start-up Pennlets (which was recently sold! It may have been ... but that's not). I love the mightytext of TechCrunch so much that I became their backstage task during the last Disrupt New York and got to with the PANTHEON of tech gods in attendance. If I were to join this , I would be a TRUE team player and work to outstanding returns.

The Path is simple, I am a Readyforce itching to get ON DECK and rockyour Dorm Room Fund.

Sincerely

Steph Weiner

smweiner@wharton.upenn.edu

Needless to say, her creativity paid off, and she was selected for the Dorm Room Fund opportunity.

Upon her return to Penn from Australia, Stephanie came back to the pressure of internship recruiting season. She interviewed for several banking, venture capital, and private equity internship opportunities. As she reflected on the experiences she enjoyed the most, her doubts dissipated as she saw more clearly that her passion was in the venture capital environment. She ended up receiving and accepting an internship offer from a venture capital firm, Insight Venture Partners. While at Insight, Stephanie was exposed to the varying stages of the start-up process and found herself most interested in the earlier stages of a start-up.

In order to secure a full-time career in venture capital upon graduation, Stephanie would attend venture capital events to make connections and learn more about the field. At one of the events, Stephanie met a few contacts she knew from her internship at the Blackstone Group, who were very supportive of her career aspirations and introduced her to Bain Capital Ventures. Through the connections made, Stephanie ended up receiving a full-time offer upon graduation.

Stephanie graduated Beta Gamma Sigma and Summa Cum Laude from the Wharton School at the University of Pennsylvania and joined Bain Capital Ventures in 2014. There were no positions readily available at the time, but because the organization was so impressed with her background and her passion, they created a role specifically for her, where she focuses on venture and growth-stage investments in technology-enabled businesses. Stephanie entered a world that traditionally requires years of experience in building numerous companies from the ground up and positioned herself perfectly for a career that invoked her interests and excited her. She succeeded in using her educational journey and experiences to try new and different things to create a career that aligned to her passion. Stephanie is a prime example of how starting early and experimenting with your interests can pay dividends towards achieving your long-term career goals.

If you could go back in time and tell the eighteen-year-old version of yourself one piece of advice for college, what would it be?

Never start an email with an apology. Your time is important, you are smart, you are worth it and no one needs to validate your efforts with your age. Stop doubting yourself, and rise to the occasion presented to you. Be confident and even fake it until you make it. In today's world that is heavily influenced by technology, a topic we know a lot about, our generation has a chance to bring value to the table. Let's take full advantage of it.

—m—

Amy Robinson
Executive Director, EyeWire

Similar to Stephanie Weiner, Amy Robinson was also named in 2015 to *Forbes'* "30 Under 30 in Games." Amy currently serves as the executive director of EyeWire, a 3D game, created by Massachusetts Institute of Technology (MIT) and Princeton researchers, which allows them to decipher how the brain processes information. Amy is also actively involved with TED and the TEDx Music Project, which she helped create.

An internship or co-op experience is a powerful way to determine what you want to do, and, equally as important, what you don't want to do. Unlike Stephanie who was trying out her interests from a very early age, Amy did not start to explore her interests outside of the classroom until her junior year internship in college. Amy put in all her effort into something that did not end up working out. This ended up setting her back, but in a good way, because it made her realize what she did not want to do for a career.

Amy grew up in Huntsville, Alabama, which has one of the highest concentrations of geospace and aerospace engineering professionals in the United

States. Growing up in this environment, she thought being an engineer would allow her to create all the cool technologies of the future. For college, she decided on Auburn University in Alabama because of its renowned engineering program. During Amy's freshman and sophomore years of college, she stayed focused on her studies and in her junior year, she was offered an engineering internship for the Department of Defense in the United States government. She was excited to finally put the things she had learned into action. To her surprise, she hated the experience; her dream job turned out to be nothing like what she had imagined. Rather than the creative, freeing, imaginative experience she dreamed of, her internship involved working in a six by six office cube being told what to do. In addition, Amy found it very disconcerting that they tested simulations of missiles. She began to think about her future and whether she wanted to spend her career trying to figure out ways to destroy things.

After leaving the internship, she was more confused about her future than ever. If her engineering experience taught her anything, it was that she needed to actually try out potential careers firsthand before committing. Searching for something new after her engineering internship, Amy changed her major first to Math, and then to Marketing. Approaching her senior year, she realized that she still had no idea what she was aiming for and started to question whether all majors would result in the same experience she had with engineering. She felt like she was going through the motions in college without a defined path and decided to take a break. Amy took a year off to get some work experience and see what was out there. She never thought that meant not returning to college. Besides the engineering internship, her only other experience to that point had come from working at Abercrombie and Fitch. Amy was hungry to find out what she was good at and what careers were out there that she would find interesting.

To start drawing on her blank sheet of paper, she got a job working for her aunt's company in environmental economics. The company bought wetlands ruined by man-made structures and then repaired those ecosystems and measured the ecological lift of the restorations in reducing toxins in the water. Amy enjoyed the job and found herself at the intersection of working with government agencies, farmers, construction companies, and venture capital firms. Her work on these complex ecosystem restoration projects fueled her curiosity about the vast complexity and interconnectedness of the planet and how her work impacted the biodiversity of the land. She decided to explore what careers existed that dealt with complex systems and networks.

Amy eventually needed a change and wanted to find projects focused on improving water quality. She started working for a nonprofit that did environmental sustainability work, which was in line with what she was seeking. At the same time, she also came across TED, a nonprofit devoted to spreading ideas, usually in the form of short, powerful talks. Amy started watching the TED events online and was instantly hooked. As she began to get more interested in the platform, her sister told her about an upcoming TEDx event in Nashville, Tennessee. TEDx events are run by independent organizers who want to create a TED-like event in their own community. Amy drove all the way to Nashville from Alabama to attend the event and fell in love with what TEDx was all about, as well as the innovative people and topics it brought together. At the event, she spontaneously decided that she wanted to create a TEDx in Huntsville, Alabama.

Amy did some research and found out that in order to have over 100 people at her events, she needed to attend an official TED conference and get a licensee to sponsor her. She found out the next big TED conference was going to be in Oxford, England, which would be a stretch for her to attend on a limited budget. She decided to turn her attention to finding a licensee for TEDx Huntsville. By searching online, she found the email of someone who previously ran one of the big TED conferences in Atlanta, Georgia. She emailed him, and the two set up a call to connect. Her goal was to see if he would be the licensee for TEDx Huntsville. The connection enjoyed talking with Amy so much that he decided to drive four hours to Huntsville to meet with her—no small commitment on his part. During lunch, she discussed the TED conference in Oxford with her new connection, and he told her she absolutely needed to go. He said it would change the scope of her ideas, the people she knew, and how she thought about the world around her. He told her to spare no expense and go. At the time, applications had already closed for the conference. Knowing Amy's desire to attend the event, her connection made some calls on her behalf and got her a spot at the conference. He also helped her get a discount on the registration fees. Amy did not have a lot of money at the time but spent every cent to get to the TED conference.

With no money in her pocket, Amy hopped on a plane to England, and was excited about what was ahead. She shared,

> The conference turned out to be everything I imagined it might be—and so much more. I was surprised to realize that the best part of TED is not the talks—they're amazing, yes—but even better are the people. Big thinkers and game changers. People from a menagerie of fields that one would likely never encounter during day-to-day activities. And since TEDTalks span virtually every subject, it has an interesting effect of breaking down people's boundaries—since these people who are used to being the experts suddenly aren't anymore, they become open minded, and playful even. Willing to talk with strangers as though they've known them for years. It's wonderful.

Now that Amy had been to a TED conference and had a licensee to support her, she was able to hold her first 100+ person TEDx event in Huntsville, Alabama. TEDx served as her outlet to have intellectual conversations with new people and get exposure to new ideas and ways of thinking. At the time, Amy's friend mentioned that she was starting a wellness division at her company, HealthSterling. Amy was looking for a change from the environmental sustainability nonprofit, and this seemed like a great opportunity. Her friend offered her a job as the creative director of HealthSterling's new wellness division.

While starting her new position at her friend's company, Amy was also creating the TEDx Music Project. At the TEDx Huntsville event, Amy hosted a performance on the evolution of Jazz which required substantial effort to produce. She began to wonder if other TEDx events were doing similar types of music presentations. She did a quick YouTube search and found all of this awesome music being produced at TEDx events. In order to bring it all together, she took the initiative to create a blog that spotlighted the top TEDx music performances. Over the next three years, it grew into a catalog of over

600 TEDx music tracks from all over the world. The growth of the initiative did not come easy, given the multiple technical and legal implications. But Amy had a vision of where she wanted this to grow to and stayed dedicated to her mission. The program has been running since 2011, and Amy now has an international team that helps her manage the project in partnership with TEDx.

Through TEDx, Amy was first exposed to crowdsourcing, the process of obtaining needed services, ideas, or content by soliciting contributions from larger groups of people. The concept intrigued her and motivated her to learn more about it. While developing crowdsourcing skills through TEDx and the TEDx Music project, she also got to take on some cool initiatives at HealthSterling, such as developing large health and corporate wellness programs. In her role as Creative Director, she would organize events such as the state's largest yoga gathering and healthy chili cook-offs. An important aspect of this was that Amy did not organize these events on her own and most of the events were not even her idea. She went up to big stakeholders and asked, "If you were going to make the city a healthier, happier place to live, what would you do?" She made it clear that they were doing events that were 100% free. The events were organized and implemented almost entirely by community members. They were truly crowdsourced initiatives, mobilizing people for a common cause.

While, Amy was balancing TEDx Huntsville, the TEDx Music Project, and the crowdsourced population health programs for HealthSterling, she was allowing herself to explore multiple interests at once. Even though she was juggling all of these competing priorities, she found time to read up on how the brain worked. She was fascinated by it, and wanted to understand how human beings functioned, made decisions, saw, and made sense of the world.

There was a neuroscientist at MIT that she had met at her first TED conference in Oxford who had given a speech about how the wiring in your brain makes you who you are. They had kept in touch over the years and Amy had come across one of his new projects, "EyeWire," on Twitter. She was inspired by the project and wrote him a note saying that she thought EyeWire would be a game changer and offered some suggestions. He wrote Amy back almost immediately and wanted to set up a Skype call to discuss her thoughts. A few weeks later, she was headed out to Palo Alto, California to a volunteer brainstorming session with EyeWire's board of directors. After the meetings, EyeWire invited Amy to come up to Boston to work on the project full time.

Six months after she sent that first email, Amy was moving to Cambridge, MA. She was now the Creative Director of a neuroscience lab and was in love with this new experience in her life. At its core, EyeWire is a scientific gaming and visualization studio which allows users to analyze neuroscience image data. When Amy started, a core problem that EyeWire had was that it could produce data much quicker than it could analyze it. There was no software in existence to quickly analyze terabytes of brain image data. Even with the best software in the world, which EyeWire has built, it takes tens of hours to analyze one neuron in the brain. The team wondered if by crowdsourcing the research they could speed up this analysis time.

They started looking at how long people spent playing games such as *Angry Birds*. They realized people were spending hours upon hours playing these games and saw it as an opportunity. A research report from 2014 showed that mobile game downloads are set to reach sixty billion worldwide by 2018.[14] To capitalize on the trend, they thought about creating a 3-D puzzle game where players mapped neurons. Amy explained, "When we first launched EyeWire, we had no idea if it would work. We hoped, but definitely didn't know." By having many users play the game, the puzzles could be solved in a record amount of time and the neuroscientists could have more answers about the brain faster than before. Essentially, they were crowdsourcing research! Since first launching, over 200,000 people worldwide have signed up to play. EyeWire is creating a neuroscience community of users that can analyze and provide input to the data sets that neuroscientists are researching.

Amy was not afraid to follow what interested her throughout her entire career. Her interests evolved, but her curiosity and ability to shift gears led her to be able to connect the dots. From engineering, to environmental work, TED, crowdsourcing, and most recently neuroscience – Amy was experimenting with careers that excited her. She is constantly learning new things and developing as a professional. Amy has spoken at numerous events in different countries ranging from TED events to the White House. In addition to being the executive director of EyeWire, Amy is now a Partner at HealthSterling. She is also still actively involved with TED through the TEDx Music Project. In addition, she continues advising the TED Prize team, attending TED events every year, and has even helped organize TED events like the first TEDx at the United Nations in New York City.

Through Amy's resilience and willingness to test out her interests, she was able to find a career that both excited and motivated her. At twenty-nine years old, Amy has accomplished a lot in her career but is still motivated to continue making an impact on the world through her work.

If you could go back in time and tell the eighteen-year-old version of yourself one piece of advice for college, what would it be?

Don't shape who you are based on what other people think is cool. Ultimately, define your own goals and interests and, if they're outside the box—good! In the future, people will love all the things you do that are different. These unique attributes will take you around the world and be amplified by your experiences—experiences which you couldn't have had if you were churning through life like everyone else.

And as for money, do you have enough to pay rent, keep the power on, get gas, and buy some decently healthy food from the grocery store? Then congrats, you're better off than about two billion people on Earth. Re-evaluate what you think is important—money only matters as much as you let it. Work without pay on projects you're passionate about and the rewards will be more amazing than your wildest dreams, which is basically priceless.

—m—

Karen Kaplan
Chairman & CEO, Hill Holliday

Karen Kaplan is the Chairman and CEO of Hill Holliday, one of the top marketing and communications agencies in the United States. She is also one of the few female agency Chairmen in the industry, and an influential leader in the Boston community. Since starting at Hill Holliday in the early 1980s as a receptionist, Karen has worked her way up the corporate ladder, working in every department of the company. Her diverse experiences within the agency help her to understand and efficiently run the overall business today. Karen was motivated by the excitement of the industry and has built a career she is very proud of.

Finding a career you are passionate about can be a long process, but sometimes you can take a chance on a new experience and fall into something you love. This was exactly the case for Karen when she took a chance on a receptionist position that turned into a long and meaningful career. Karen grew up in Marblehead, Massachusetts, in a middle class family with one older sister and two working parents. Her mother empowered Karen and her sister to dream big; she wanted her girls to know that they could do anything they set their minds to.

Karen and her sister were the first two in the family to attend college. Karen graduated fifth in her class in high school and applied (and was later accepted) early decision to Colby College in Waterville, Maine. She declared English as her major since at the time, that was what she thought she wanted to study. After her freshman year, she realized that Colby was too small for her and that she needed a change. She transferred to the University of Massachusetts Amherst (UMass Amherst) and was excited about the new opportunity to meet new people and explore new ideas. The school had much more diverse language programs so she switched from English to French Literature. She had always wanted to study in Europe, and, at the time, only language students had the opportunity to study abroad.

Karen decided to study abroad in both Madrid, Spain, and in a small town just outside of Paris, France, for her entire junior year. While abroad, she also started a small business to make some extra money. She put signs in all of the apartment buildings in the town she was staying in and tutored others in speaking English. Her study abroad experience was a tremendous growth opportunity for her and gave her a chance to have a different perspective on the world.

After graduation and her experience abroad, she was eager to get out in the world and experience new and different things. She did not do a formal internship during college, as most companies did not offer them at the time. During the summers, she did, however, work as a waitress on Cape Cod, MA, to get some work experience and earn some extra money for school. Karen's college experience was unique and rewarding. Without realizing it, she had started experimenting with her talents and interests, and she was almost ready to map out a plan for her future. She admitted, "I decided where I was going to college originally for all the wrong reasons, but ended up with a patchwork quilt of a really great college experience in the end."

After graduating from UMass Amherst in the early 1980s, the US economy was in a recession. The unemployment rate was in the double digits and graduating college with a job was nearly impossible. As an alternative, Karen started thinking about going to law school as a next step. She figured that a law degree would always come in handy and that it would buy her some time until the job market improved. While babysitting and waitressing for money, she was also feeling out the job market before committing to law school. Her sister put her in touch with a recruiter who told her about a receptionist position that was available at Hill Holliday, an advertising agency in Boston. Karen thought this could be a great opportunity for her. It would be a true nine to five job, which would allow her time to study for the LSATs and apply to law schools.

She soon found out that Jack Connors, one of the founders of Hill Holliday, was personally interviewing all candidates. Jack Connors was a celebrity in Boston, and Karen was motivated to take advantage of the opportunity to interview with him. She was told he had already interviewed and rejected over forty candidates, and she wanted to be the one to get this opportunity. Her first time in a business environment was during her interview at Hill Holliday. She had some biases that the business world was suits and ties and dominated by male egos. However, when she got off the elevator for her interview, she was pleasantly surprised. She saw many young people working in a truly diverse environment. It was a cool, idea-driven culture that was wild in every sense of the word. It was work hard, play hard, and completely not what she expected of the business world. After her interview, she was hired almost immediately.

When she was hired, Jack said to her "Congratulations, Karen. You are now the face and the voice of Hill Holliday". This gave her pause because she thought that "the face and the voice" was what the CEO should be. She quickly learned that Jack Connors took her position very seriously, so she did as well. She decided that she was the CEO of the reception desk, and from that moment on, used this frame of mind when approaching every job after that. Karen fell in love with the job and the company. After her first year, law school was out the window and she was looking for a way to advance her career. She applied to a few secretary positions and got rejected because she didn't have the necessary technical skills. However, with perseverance, she was able to get an assistant position in the Traffic Department.

The Traffic Department handled project management and administrative work for the entire company. The role was pivotal for her because she got to work with every single department throughout the entire agency. Her first two positions as receptionist and Traffic Assistant gave her great perspective on the inner workings of the entire agency. One requirement of the Traffic Assistant position was to produce a report and have it on everyone's desk by 8:00 am Monday morning. The only problem was, Karen didn't know how to type. The department only had one word processor at the time and it was right outside her boss's office. Not wishing her boss to know that it took her all day to type the report, she would come in on Saturdays and Sundays to do the work. One weekend, while producing the report, Karen found a pay sheet with senior executives' names on it, jammed inside the copy machine. Karen had no idea people made that kind of money; she was making $12,500 and hoped to get to $15,000! Seeing the earning potential within the company motivated Karen to work even harder, especially since she enjoyed what she was doing.

She later transitioned into account management which encompassed all the client-facing activities of the agency. After having two internal roles, Karen saw this as a great opportunity to learn more about how the agency interacted with its clients. She continued to advance while hitting a key milestone in her life of becoming a mother. Upon returning from maternity leave, Karen had a desire to be around for her family and knew that she could not be traveling for work. She opted to become the director of the Design Department so she could juggle her two jobs – being a mom and an employee of Hill Holiday. As Director, she was responsible for the operations and Profit and Loss (P&L) of her business line. She learned financial management and managerial skills that would later be vital in her future roles.

As the company continued to rapidly grow, Karen would take on pitches as side projects when she had time. If Hill Holliday won a pitch, and Karen was an assistant account executive, they would put her on the staffing plan as an account executive. These side projects helped Karen accelerate her development. Through the company's growth, she was propelled forward. Over the course of her twenty plus year career, Karen has had twelve different jobs at Hill Holliday; taking on a new position every two years due to the rapid growth of the agency. Hill Holiday allowed Karen to explore multiple different interests during her career within one company. In December 2000, Karen's first taste of agency management came when she got promoted to Managing Director of the Boston office. Due to the dot com bubble, the agency had a lot of technology clients at the time. When the tech bubble burst in February of 2001, Karen was left holding unrealistic forecasts made by prior management. She felt blindsided, and then September 11th happened later that year. She told us, "2001, I always say, was my management boot camp. You learn a lot more in the bad times than you do in the good times." It was time for Karen to earn her stripes in agency management and she did so very gracefully, leading Hill Holliday through very challenging times.

Staying at one company for an entire career is not the norm today and was not necessarily the norm when Karen entered the workforce either. She stumbled into the perfect environment that allowed her to try different things, show her interest and potential, and be successful. Since starting at Hill Holliday, Karen has had jobs in every single product category that the company serves. Karen is now the Chairman and CEO of Hill Holliday and has been a driving force in Hill Holliday's growth to more than $1 billion in revenue. She has been recognized as one of the most influential women in advertising and serves on the Board of Directors for numerous civic and professional organizations. From receptionist to CEO of one of the world's largest advertising agencies, Karen Kaplan has proved there are many paths to the top. Karen acknowledges the relationship between hard work and passion and reminds us, "I haven't slept in thirty-three years but it was because I loved what I was doing every day and always wanted to take on more." Don't be afraid to try new opportunities as they come up, you never know where they will lead.

If you could go back in time and tell the eighteen-year-old version of yourself one piece of advice for college, what would it be?

Don't look at failure as a bad thing. You either win or you learn; no one ever made progress by playing it safe.

—m—

John Harthorne
CEO and Founder of MassChallenge

John Harthorne is the CEO and Founder of MassChallenge, the world's largest start-up accelerator. Since MassChallenge was established in Boston, Massachusetts in 2010, it has succeeded in launching 617 start-ups and has raised over $947 million in funding.[15] The organization has now expanded internationally and is having an impact across the world. In 2013, John was voted Social Entrepreneur of the Year in New England by Ernst & Young and elected as one of the 2013 Young Global Leaders by the World Economic Forum. He was also identified as one of Boston's 50 Most Influential Business Leaders by the *Boston Business Journal*. If you have heard of John Harthorne, you have probably heard of his philanthropic success and marveled at his passion and originality. Like many of us, John was once lost too, and was uncertain about his future. It took John many years after college to find a career that he was passionate about and that would challenge him to bring out the best in himself.

John grew up in Wayland, MA, and attended Deerfield Academy, a private boarding school in Deerfield, MA. During his first year, John ranked in the top 5% of his class and had one of the highest GPAs in the entire school. However, John was later exposed to many distractions which held him back from progressing in his studies. After graduating from Deerfield Academy, John began his college career at Bowdoin College in Maine, where his behavior did not differ much from high school in terms of the vices that occupied his time. He was an average student at best with grades in the C range. Apart from a few classes, John felt that he did not learn much while in college, but remarked, "This is where I should have been figuring out who I was and what I wanted to do with my life." Does John's narrative sound familiar so far? If so, his narrative can provide a valuable lesson on how to not go through the motions in college, expecting that it will all come together after graduation.

As graduation approached, John began to notice his peers had lined up full-time jobs. He found himself thinking, *When did these guys get jobs? When was I supposed to do that?* John realized he had done nothing in preparation to secure a full-time job after college and began to panic. Finally, with graduation right around the corner, he came across a program posted at school that provided the opportunity to earn a master's degree in Europe. He applied for the program, gaining acceptance to obtain his master's degree in European Political Culture in England and Berlin. After two years in the graduate program, John moved back to the United States and was eager to start drawing on a blank sheet of paper to find a career he was passionate about. He interned, without pay, with the United Nations in New York as a translator and, like too many college graduates, worked simply to get by.

A few years later, in 1998, John decided that he needed to reset and headed back to Boston to re-evaluate where his life was headed. Upon his return, John was able to find himself a job, translating automobile repair manuals from German to English. While working, he avidly searched for other careers paths by talking to people and reading as much as he could. The idea of consulting intrigued him, as he felt he was a reasonably smart guy who could learn quickly and help solve complicated problems. However, he also quickly learned that most large consulting firms only hired the best students from the top schools, a major roadblock for John as his own grades were not good enough for him to be considered for an interview. He had set his mind on this career path, and knew he could find an alternative way to break into this competitive industry, leading him to consider business school as an option. He began to map out a plan of action for how to show his qualifications based on his experiences rather than academics.

The early 2000's Internet boom inspired John to consider careers in this growing field. He had always considered himself somewhat of a computer geek, as he had been exposed to computers at a very young age. While traveling, John met a woman on a flight back to Boston from Amsterdam that connected him with his next job opportunity at a digital security consulting start-up in Cambridge, MA. The thought of a start-up company excited John, and he felt it would be a great opportunity to test out this type of career. Their dialogue led the woman to offer John an interview where he would later be offered a full-time position.

With the thought of business school still in mind, he knew that his new job at the technology start-up would be helpful for a variety of reasons. He hoped the job would give him some much needed management experience, and the location was also a bonus as it was in Kendall Square in Cambridge, MA, just blocks away from the prestigious Massachusetts Institute of Technology (MIT) Sloan School of Management, where he had dreamed of going for his MBA. John also loved that he was now working in a rapidly growing industry where he could learn a variety of new skills. He loved the start-up environment, the culture, and the people with whom he was working. For once, he was enjoying going into work every day.

A newlywed at this time, John came home one day from work to find his wife in tears because she was homesick. They decided they should move to his wife's home country of Russia for a year to reset. He pictured his wife being happier and knew they would have the opportunity to travel, visit interesting places, and he would have the opportunity to finally focus on business school applications. John wasn't afraid to draw on a blank sheet of paper and explore different opportunities in his life when they came up.

In Russia, he was able to self-reflect on what he truly valued in life which helped him gain focus and allowed him to start making intentional decisions about his career. By the time he was finally accepted to MIT's MBA program in 2005, he was truly engaged in his coursework, attending every class, and fully participating; ultimately becoming one of the top performers in his class. His vision from years prior had become a reality. This increased focus was all due to realizing his values and what activities motivated him. He further crystallized his path and decided to hone in on start-ups and strategy consulting as the careers he wanted to pursue.

During his time at MIT Sloan, John involved himself in the community as well, and ended up winning the 2007 MIT $100K business plan competition. Along with two other students, he also ran the largest start-up conference ever held at the school to promote entrepreneurship on campus and abroad. Although he longed to jump right into entrepreneurship, he had $150,000 worth of debt and was married with a child. He thought he had no choice but to go and work for a company that would provide him with a stable income. Student loans forced him to delay a career aspiration of being an entrepreneur. He interned at Bain and Company during one of his summers at MIT and decided to accept a full-time offer with the consulting firm upon graduation. Through hard work and dedication, he had made his vision of attending MIT and getting a job in strategy consulting a reality. However, while John was successful at Bain and learned a tremendous amount, he confirmed that a career in strategy consulting was not his true passion.

In December 2008, amidst the largest economic collapse of his lifetime, he realized that his dream of creating a start-up was going to be setback even further. One night, he remembered a quote that he felt reflected what made America great: "Give me your tired, your poor, your huddled masses yearning to breathe free, the wretched refuse of your teeming shore. Send these, the homeless, tempest-tossed, to me: I lift my lamp beside the golden door." Emma Lazarus's famous words are written on a plaque at the base of the Statue of Liberty and symbolize the foundation of American culture. He began to view the world as a larger opportunity to solve problems and create solutions to promote optimism, hope, growth, and forward-thinking ideas. This was his "ah-ha" moment.

John realized that any organization had two fundamental responsibilities to society: (1) creating value for others and (2) capturing some of that value to sustain one's own organization. In comparing value to a pie, the individual running the organization has to ensure that customers, employees, suppliers, society, the government, and the organization itself each have a slice of the pie. One of the important lessons that he learned in business school was how one can maximize the size of their personal slice, regardless of the impact on others' slices. John questioned this notion by asking, *Why can't we make more pie as a society instead of everyone competing for a bigger piece?* He wanted to restore creativity to the soul of the economy by making innovation and value creation the ultimate goal, instead of profit.

John woke up that next morning with an adrenaline rush, realizing he could be a potential solution to this problem. "Wasn't that part of the problem?" he recalled. "Nobody was doing anything about it." John reflected on his experiences: he attended MIT Sloan, received awards for entrepreneurship, and ran a conference fostering entrepreneurial activity and economic value by using catalytic events such as competitions. He realized this could be an answer to the problem. America built a reputation for having the best innovation ecosystem on the planet, so why not build a competition to use that strength for the greater good? The competition would challenge entrepreneurs to bring out their best ideas and be provided with everything they needed (money, office space, media support, etc.) to bring it to reality. He found his passion and gave birth to the mission of MassChallenge: to catalyze a global renaissance.

Since its formation, MassChallenge has created 5,100 jobs for the economy through the 617 start-ups they have helped launch.[16] Although John didn't find a career he was passionate about in college, he kept drawing on a blank sheet of paper until he founded MassChallenge. Finding careers that motivate and excite you is difficult and does not happen overnight; however, the sooner you can get started, the sooner you can find one.

If you could go back in time and tell the eighteen-year-old version of yourself one piece of advice for college, what would it be?

I remember this quote from a song, "Wear with pride the scars on your skin, to remember the people and places you've been." If I had not messed up so many times, I don't know that I would have gotten to where I am today. However, it would have been nice to have found my passions earlier. You need to take life a little more seriously while in college and place an emphasis on discovering your values. There should be a focus on your skills to accomplish your goals, but what really matters is finding out what you want to do with those skills and why. You need to find what really matters to you and what you care about. Once you finally arrive at a place of choice where you have the ability to decide what you want, it is the most powerful place you could ever be in. The goal you should seek to accomplish is to have the control to know where you are going and why.

—⟋⟍—

Putting Pen To Paper

Reflect on Stephanie, Amy, Karen and John's experiences and think about how you can start drawing on a blank sheet of paper to zero in on your career.

In order to get started in experimenting with careers, make sure you are utilizing all the tools available to you. A key characteristic of all great leaders is resourcefulness. You don't have to figure it all out on your own; leverage the tools, people, and support systems around you.

(1) **Career Services:** Set up a one-on-one meeting with your career counselor, and learn about all the resources available to you. Career service departments can typically help with resume and cover letter critiques, internship and co-op opportunities the school has with different employers, and other career development opportunities. Some colleges have job shadow programs where students can go to organizations and learn about what it is like to work there. Some also have internship sponsorship programs whereby students can get paid for unpaid

internships. Be sure you are utilizing all that your school is giving you to maximize your investment.

(2) Clubs & Organizations: Stephanie Weiner was able to find a career she was passionate about in college partly through her participation in several clubs and organizations on campus. Her experience in the Entrepreneurship club and running the Dorm Room Fund confirmed Stephanie's interest in venture capital. By the time she got the offer from Bain Capital Ventures, she knew it was the right career for her and would excel based on her experiences. Talk to your friends on campus, career services, your professors, and other resources to get a full inventory of what clubs and organizations exist at your school. Once you find a few that interest you, reach out to the organizer or leader and ask to learn more; for instance, see if they have an information session coming up that you could attend. If you can't find the exact club you were looking for to explore your interests, create one. Develop your idea, get feedback from others, build a community around it, work with your college to get support, and establish it.

(3) Internships & Co-ops: Internships and co-ops are the best ways to experience a career firsthand without fully committing years of your life. Internship and co-op experiences put students in roles that resemble a full-time employee, and many of these programs typically lead to employment offers after graduation. Because internships and co-ops are such great opportunities to learn and experience a career, program acceptance is highly competitive. Securing an internship with one of the top companies, organizations, or government agencies is a vision for many students starting out in college. Career services is a good place to start to determine which employers your school has recruiting relationships with. Learn about when they come to campus for interviews and what they require. You can also go on a potential employer's website yourself and learn about what internship or co-op opportunities exist, when they are offered, and what they look for in applicants. This way, you can start mapping out the qualifications you will need before you apply.

One challenge you may discover is that most of these formal opportunities are only available once students are juniors. Typically, employers already want to see some formal employment and leadership experience on candidates' resumes. In order to start getting experience sooner, you can find internship-type opportunities at smaller local employers and nonprofits. These local employers are looking for young talent who can help them stay on top of current trends. When searching for internship opportunities, also look for "part-time" opportunities and "unpaid internships." By understanding your options to get experience, you can determine which opportunity works best for your schedule. Money is very important, but do not underestimate the value of the right experience and how it can pay off in the future.

(4) **Leadership Development & Diversity Programs:** Many top employers offer leadership development and diversity programs. Research and check your eligibility. These programs vary by employer and can either be one- or two-day events, a week-long immersion program, or a semester-long opportunity. Check in with career services to see what types of opportunities they know about. You can also go online to see if other employers you are interested in offer similar opportunities. These programs are great ways to test out careers and companies on a small scale. Many of these programs are also designed for freshman and sophomore students to act as a feeder program for their internships.

(5) **Campus Employment & Leadership Programs:** Explore what opportunities your school offers for part-time employment during the school year. For instance, if you were interested in finance or accounting, your school may offer campus employment in the accounts payable department. Colleges also typically offer leadership and honors programs for their high-achieving students. Learn about the requirements and apply. These leadership and honors programs make you stand out from your peers and give you access to resources that other students don't have like honors networking events.

(6) **Study Abroad Programs:** Learn about what study abroad opportunities are available to you that you would be interested in. While fun and enriching, spending time abroad will also grow your understanding of various cultures and differentiate you from your peers. Study abroad and alternative spring break programs broaden your perspective on how the world works. Use these opportunities to get outside

of your comfort zone and see new places. Stephanie, Karen, and John all experienced different study abroad programs which helped them think differently about their career and their life choices.

(7) **Events and Conferences:** This is a great segue to our next chapter on making connections; conference and events both on and off campus are tremendous learning experiences and can open up your perspective on different careers. After Amy Robinson found TED and went to her first event in Oxford, England, she was hooked. John Harthorne also started an Entrepreneurship conference when he attended MIT which would later give him the idea for MassChallenge. Do some research on potential events and conferences that you might want to attend and find out when they are on or off campus each semester. Get smart on the conference and event topics and speakers to maximize your experience. If you can't find a conference you're interested in, start one.

Make the conscious effort to try new and different things, get out of your comfort zone, and draw on your blank sheet of paper to create a picture of your future worth more to you than a paycheck.

CHAPTER 3
Making Connections

"Trust is the glue of life. It's the most essential
ingredient in effective communication. It's the
foundational principle that holds all relationships."[17]
- STEPHEN COVEY, AUTHOR OF *7 HABITS*
OF HIGHLY EFFECTIVE PEOPLE

H as anyone ever told you, "It's all about who you know?" Likely, at one point in your life, a connection has provided you with a beneficial opportunity. Human connections are what drive this world and everything in it. All of the world's biggest companies, organizations, and government agencies are a collection of people, all performing tasks and duties for a common purpose. There are over seven billion people on earth today, and that number is only set to rise as the world continues to develop. Start approaching every encounter with a new person as an opportunity to showcase who you are and what you are all about. The relationships you build with others will allow you to plug into their diverse networks and can lead to new opportunities, ideas, and connections—if you go about building relationships the right way.

Whether it's family, friends, classmates, colleagues, or teammates, the majority of each day is spent seeing, listening to, and interacting with other people. Many of us do not consciously think about what we are trying to get out of these daily interactions. Without having some sort of focus, we cannot be sure that the connections we are making are the right ones. This chapter is meant to show you how to consciously think about your network and make connections in a more productive way.

By experimenting with different careers first-hand, you will inevitably meet new people. These interactions will enable you to find people you want to emulate and discover communities and groups you want to join.[18] You will begin to notice certain characteristics in the people you admire most. Pay attention to the way they carry themselves, present material, approach solving complex problems, or their dedication to their organization or team. These are personal attributes that you consider valuable. Define what characteristics you value so that you can connect with others whose values align with yours. You want to focus on the connections you have made with people who support who you are and what you are trying to accomplish.

To ensure you are making the right connections and building the right support system, evaluate your values regularly. Think for a minute about what you value most. We have provided a few examples to get you started.

Examples:

(1) *Dependable—always being the person people can count on.*

(2) *Giving—enjoy giving back and making a difference in the lives of others.*

(3) *Caring—enjoy spending time with and supporting my family and closest friends.*

(4) *Adventurous—always looking to travel, try new things, and solve tough problems.*

(5) *Healthy—enjoy staying physically and mentally fit.*

Once you have defined your values, take your goals into consideration. Values tell others about your personal characteristics and strengths; however, for connections to be effective, conveying your goals is just as important. By telling others what you are striving for, they will get a better picture of how they can help and support you in accomplishing your objectives. Do you know what your top goals are?

Examples:

(1) Get straight As both Fall and Spring semester.

(2) Find a way to get job experience in Digital Marketing.

(3) Get more familiar with the legal profession by joining the law club, reading more, and going to industry events.

(4) Get a paid internship for the upcoming summer.

(5) Take Mandarin classes to learn Chinese and learn more about business trends in Asia.

Now that you have your values and goals defined, you can start to take a look at your network to ensure you're investing in the right relationships to find your career. To make this easier, your network can be broken up into manageable groups which can provide more structure for getting the most out of new and existing connections (see Figure 2).

Figure 2:

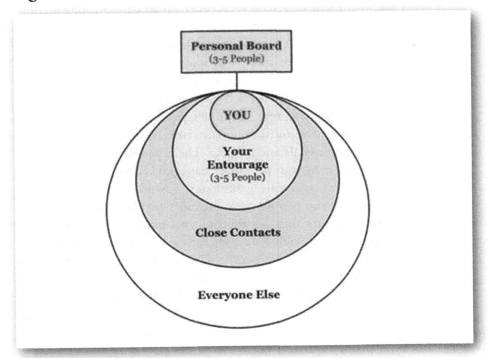

(1) **Personal Board:** Do you know what a board of directors is? It is a group of individuals who are elected to serve as the governing body of a corporation or organization. Similar to how companies need guidance and support from their board to make sure they are taking the right steps forward—so do you. Your personal board should be a group of influential individuals who are the primary support system and sounding board for your career. These are people you emulate and who are extremely well connected within the community. You want your personal board to be a diverse group of individuals covering multiple industries and having different experiences. As you test your interests to find your passions, these individuals can open doors you never thought existed. Think of these individuals as your mentors,

people you trust, and people who have your back. Actively stay in contact with them and keep each other up to date on information, ideas, and opportunities where possible. Since this group requires regular communication, it is typically not large, and as a rule of thumb, should be between three and five people.

(2) **Your Entourage:** Have you seen the HBO series *Entourage*? Vince, Drama, E, and Turtle never left each other's side on their rise to the top of Hollywood. Your entourage represents those people with whom you have the most frequent contact, and who are closely aligned with your goals and values.[19] These people may not be as influential as those in your personal board but represent close friends, family members, mentors, teammates, coworkers, professors, etc. Since these are the people who are most involved with your life, take time to ensure they are the right people, and that they are in full support of your objectives. Has anyone ever told you that you are the average of the five people with whom you spend the most time? Surround yourself with the right people who will lift you up and push you to your highest potential. Leverage your entourage by bouncing ideas off of them and asking for advice. Similar to your personal board, consider keeping your entourage to between three and five people.

(3) **Close Contacts:** Your close contacts are those people whom you have met through life experiences but who you do not connect with as frequently as your personal board and your entourage. Close contacts are very valuable to you because they typically are more diverse than your entourage and can provide you with new ideas, information, perspectives, and connections.[20] It is important to not let these relationships run dry. It is difficult, if not impossible, to manage all of your close contacts efficiently. Take advantage of select opportunities to re-engage and keep the relationship warm. Find ways to update each other on new developments and how you might be able to support each other going forward. Use technology and social media to your benefit. Shoot someone a quick text or email when you think of them, or tag them in a social media post that they may also enjoy.

(4) Everyone Else: Like the name suggests, everyone else encompasses the seven billion plus other people on this planet that you may connect with during your lifetime. Each interaction with a new person is a learning opportunity. By meeting new and diverse people, we expose ourselves to a variety of new ideas, thoughts, connections, and opportunities. Take the time to listen to others, get to know them, and see what you can learn from them that might help you in your journey to find a career. Oftentimes, some of the best connections we have made in our lives were from random encounters.

If we meet someone who seems aligned with our values and goals, it might wise to develop the relationship further and see what opportunities or additional connections you both can share. One of the key characteristics of successful people is their ability to bridge multiple networks and help each other. Think about it, if a friend helped you by connecting you with someone in their network, wouldn't you be more likely to help them somewhere down the line? A "friend of a friend" and other random people we meet every day are sometimes the most beneficial to us in achieving our goals and transforming our careers. Take time to plant seeds with everyone you meet by making a positive impression and being grounded in who you are (your values) and what you are trying to accomplish (your goals).

In order to get started on structuring and defining your network, start by thinking about who the three to five people are that you would consider part of your personal board. What is the current status of your relationship? How are you going to develop that relationship further? Is there a certain type of person that needs to be added to your personal board?

Once you have defined your personal board, you can use the same process to define your entourage. Start to challenge and test the connections you have in your network to make sure they are the right ones. Determine which relationships have escaped you and require some investment of your time. It is important to evaluate your network of connections at least twice a year and decide whether changes need to be made. Assess whether connections need to be swapped, moved, added, or removed. Yes, relationships do need to be removed at times. As your values and goals change, some relationships are bound to move out of alignment. Alternatively, certain relationships may no longer be reciprocating benefits to you, even though you are sharing information, ideas, and connections with them. You want your network to be as relevant as possible to ensure you are maximizing your career opportunities and have the right support system. Don't be afraid to cut a connection loose if it is holding you back.

Many college students think of making connections as "networking." The theory behind networking is that the more contacts you have, the more opportunity you will have for one of them to pay off.[21] Students who take this approach end up with redundant connections (i.e., same industry or field) because they are not intentionally searching for the right connections.[22] Each connection is thought of only in the context of how it benefits you (i.e., getting an internship or job). Networking in theory sounds great, but it doesn't work in practice. It creates one-sided relationships where you are only trying to get an immediate benefit out of the other person. Eventually, that connection will realize it is a one-sided relationship and that they are being used.[23] Making connections is different from networking and is built on the exchange of mutual trust, benefit, and ideas.

So how do you build connections? In today's global world, everyone is on the move. We connect with others mostly via technology, including through email, teleconferencing, cell phones, and social media. Although there is still no substitute for connecting in person to build rapport, many people are too busy balancing multiple priorities. Be efficient when building connections to ensure you're maximizing your time. To help you get started in making connections with others and turning them into trusting relationships, you can follow a few guiding principles.

(1) **Keep an Open Mind:** Many students mistakenly think that they can only build connections during networking events, internships, or other formal, "professional" settings. In fact, some of the best opportunities to make strong connections come outside of these formal settings. Working out at the gym, attending a sporting event,

or even getting your morning coffee at Starbucks are sometimes the best places to develop connections because people have their guard down. Many times, the setting also helps to establish that you have common values and interests. For instance, introducing yourself to someone at the gym immediately tells them that you also enjoy working out. Make time to get out there and interact with everyone else. Connecting with people outside your typical "comfort zone" provides you with a variety of fresh ideas and information which allows you to broaden your perspectives. Similar to how salesmen track "leads," your interactions with everyone else are potential opportunities that you can benefit from in both small and big ways. When meeting new people, be focused on ways you can build your credibility and their trust.

(2) **Ask Opened-Ended Questions:** When meeting someone for the first time, or when reconnecting with a close contact, ask open-ended questions. These types of questions often start with "how," "what," or "why," and invite collaboration and the sharing of information or ideas. You want your connections to share as much information with you as possible. By getting your connections to open up, you can better understand their values, goals, current opportunities, and challenges. This puts you in a better position to share relevant information and ideas to strengthen the relationship.

(3) **Establish Common Ground:** When making connections, it is very important to establish your credibility and commonality with the other person. This doesn't mean bragging about yourself. It means honestly communicating your strengths, accomplishments, and unique experiences.[24] By establishing your credibility and commonality, and by showcasing what you are capable of, you are introducing the value you can bring to your connection. This common bond tells your connection that you are like them, and strengthens the relationship over time.

(4) **Maintain and Strengthen the Relationship:** The best relationships are built on trust and the only way to build trusting relationships is through the constant exchange of ideas, information, support, and other connections over time. Invest time to consistently maintain and strengthen your relationships. The focus is on mutual benefits rather

than individual needs.[25] The amount of time you dedicate to each connection depends on where they sit in your network.

(5) **Don't Be Afraid to Ask for Help:** You are not alone in your journey toward finding a career you are passionate about. When you are uncertain and need some guidance, leverage your network and in particular your personal board and entourage. Bounce ideas, concerns, decisions, and questions off of these connections for feedback and recommendations. Just remember, you also need to be there for your connections when they need support to maintain a mutually beneficial relationship. Working through issues, concerns, and big decisions with your connections shows that you are there for them and strengthens the trust in the relationship.

This world is too big and complex to go after your career goals and dreams alone. Get others to buy into your vision and leverage them to make the journey easier. Through some series of connections, commonly referred to as six degrees of separation, we are connected to almost everyone on this planet. Start defining, managing, and strengthening your relationships in college to position yourself for post-graduate success.

The next section of this chapter will introduce you to four more individuals who have used their network effectively to build strong mutually beneficial relationships that created life-changing opportunities. Learn from their experiences and advice and think about what actions you can take to make effective connections with others who can support the goals you are trying to achieve.

—⟋⟍—

Daniel Koh
Chief of Staff City of Boston

On December 8th, 2015, while we were writing this book, one of the headlines on Boston.com read, "This is the most powerful 30-year-old in Boston."[26] The article was referencing Daniel Koh, the Chief of Staff to Marty Walsh, the Mayor of the City of Boston. Daniel is a World Economic Forum Global Shaper, has spoken at TEDx, and has accomplished a tremendous amount in his short career. Along the path to finding his passion for public service, Daniel also worked at a recruiting company, explored a career in baseball management, and worked in the media and entertainment industry. Throughout his career, Daniel has built strong relationships that have opened up doors for him. Finding a career that motivates you is rarely a solo act and involves interpersonal skills and social networking.

Daniel grew up in Andover, Massachusetts, in a very public service-oriented family. His father was the Commissioner of Public Health for Massachusetts from 1997–2003 and before that was heavily involved in the anti-tobacco movement. Thanks to his father's social connections, Daniel had the opportunity to be part of an undercover sting operation concerning unlawful sales of cigarettes to minors. Driving with a police officer in an unmarked vehicle, Daniel tried to buy cigarettes from local vendors. He was underage, and looked young, and Daniel knew store owners should not even consider selling him cigarettes, but to his surprise, he had no trouble buying them.

Two years later, Daniel attended a hearing on whether or not to ban smoking in Andover's restaurants and bars. At the end of the hearing, he was eager to voice his opinion, despite being too young to vote. The Board of Health could not come to a clear decision on the matter. Daniel decided to put his fears aside and raise his hand. When called, he bravely spoke,

> As a young kid, we don't always want to admit we are looking up to older people, but we are. And when we see people smoking in restaurants we think that is the acceptable behavior of what you should do when you go out to eat. I get nervous about us not passing this because I think the impression it leaves on kids is formidable.

The Board ended up enacting the smoking ban in Andover and cited Daniel's testimonial as one of the main reasons why. For Daniel, this was an important lesson about making an impact on the health and lives of others in his hometown.

In high school, Daniel interned for Senator Ted Kennedy. He would watch the ongoing affairs of the United States Senate on TV, and at work he would then interact with those who were stakeholders in the present issues. Daniel thoroughly enjoyed being in on the action and feeling like he was making a difference for the greater good of society.

Upon graduating from high school, Daniel attended Harvard University for his undergraduate degree. During the spring semester of his freshman year, he learned through his network of a fellowship program where a select number of students would be paired up with politicians. Daniel applied to the program and was fortunate enough to be selected. He was paired up with Jesse "The Body" Ventura, a former wrestler and navy seal, now turned politician. It was an enlightening experience for Daniel that provided him with different perspectives on public service. During his time at Harvard, Daniel also interned for Ted Kennedy twice more and started to realize his interest in the public sector had become a passion.

Upon graduating from Harvard, Daniel started looking for his next opportunity and got his first full-time job at Spencer Stuart, one of the world's leading global executive search firms. He found it to be a little less sexy than he expected but learned how to search for executives' email addresses using search keys on Google. Daniel used this skill going forward to connect with people from different companies and organizations to establish relationships and build his network.

After about four months, Daniel realized that he wanted to explore another interest of his, strategy consulting. Through a connection, he was fortunate enough to be referred to Booz Allen Hamilton, where he worked for a year and a half. At the start of his time there, he enjoyed the experience but missed the public sector work he grew up loving. Daniel came across a partner of the firm aligned to the nonprofit sector and reached out to him via email multiple times until he finally was able to introduce himself and form a connection. Realizing his passion and commitment, this partner put him in touch with someone who was able to staff Daniel on a nonprofit project. By taking a chance and reaching out, Daniel was able to create an opportunity for himself.

While working on the nonprofit project, Daniel found out that he was accepted into Harvard Business School to earn his MBA. Wanting to try something new before business school, he started looking for other opportunities to further his passions. One of his college classmates had worked for the Vice President of Business Development for the New England Patriots football team. Daniel had previously met her, and kept in touch with her over the years. After reaching out to her and expressing interest in working for her, she helped Daniel get an internship in their strategy and ticketing department until classes started. By rekindling a connection from his past, Daniel had found another exciting internship opportunity. He left Booz Allen Hamilton, and during his internship helped the Patriots develop their Twitter page and create strategies for their new ticketing platform to increase sales.

Being a first-year MBA student, Daniel applied to all of the strategy and management consulting firms that offered opportunities on campus during the fall, and while he interviewed and completed countless case studies, he was not extended an offer by any of the firms he applied to. Daniel felt the pressure to make something happen to advance his career. Through the Business of Sports Club network, he learned that the MLB Commissioner's Office was hiring an intern for the Labor Relations Department, a group that acts as an internal consultancy for teams when determining how much to pay a player. Daniel interviewed, was offered the job, and immediately moved to New York City despite making very little money. The job aligned directly with Daniel's interest in both sports and consulting, and he often stayed late at work reading up on ESPN and putting in extra hours.

After his internship with the Commissioner's office, Daniel was eager to look for new opportunities to get back into the public sector. Upon returning to Harvard for his second year of business school, he learned of a program for graduates offering a salary for a variety of different public sector and nonprofit jobs. One such job was for the Mayor's office in Boston working for Tom Menino, who had been in office for eighteen years and still stands as the longest running mayor in Boston's history. Daniel was offered a job that involved enhancing the Mayor's social media presence and boosting the summer jobs program for the City of Boston. This program hires approximately 10,000 Boston public school students every year to a number of private sector and nonprofit jobs. Daniel helped the team create a website to assist in marketing the program and signed up 300 new company partnerships.

Growing up, he had also always been interested in the media industry, including different forms of entertainment and sharing of information. During his time at business school at Harvard University, there was a case study on the *Huffington Post*. Arianna Huffington, editor and chief of the *Huffington Post*, encouraged students to start their own blogs if inspired to do so. Daniel took the initiative to email Arianna to connect. He wanted to learn more about blogging and by sending the email, was able to get a position.

Daniel was still interested in strategy consulting and continued to look for opportunities. After learning of an upcoming position for hire, he applied, and also connected with an employee of the firm to meet over coffee and learn more about the potential position. The consultant was impressed that Daniel was blogging for the *Huffington Post* and mentioned that it was something he had always wanted to try. Daniel connected him with the editor and shortly thereafter he was offered a full-time position. Unfortunately, Daniel did not receive an offer for the job at the consulting firm as he had hoped.

About nine months later, Daniel received a call back from that same consultant saying thank you, and that he had never forgotten Daniel's favor. He mentioned Arianna Huffington was looking for a new Chief of Staff and asked if Daniel was interested. The relationship had finally reciprocated. Daniel applied and was offered the position, requiring him to return to New York City. He worked for Arianna for a year and a half and developed tremendous skills in this time period. Arianna was not only the editor-in-chief of a hugely successful online magazine, but she was also an icon. Daniel was responsible for helping her run the business on the ground, but also had to coordinate with her while she was traveling.

While serving as Arianna's Chief of Staff, the company launched their streaming network, *HuffPost Live*, and was in need of a general manager who knew the business. After holding his Chief of Staff role for a year and half, Daniel wanted to challenge himself to try something new, and believed he was qualified for the *HuffPost Live* position. He conveyed his goals in a candid conversation with Arianna, and she gave him the opportunity. The experience was incredible for Daniel and he felt like he was truly running a business.

During his time at the *Huffington Post*, Daniel had kept in touch with Mitch Weiss, then Mayor Menino's Chief of Staff for the City of Boston. He had first met Mitch when he worked for Thomas Menino, and Mitch liked and respected Daniel, resulting in a lasting relationship between the two of them. He had been following the political scene and knew Mayor Walsh had just been elected as the new Mayor of Boston. Soon after, Mitch called Daniel, informing him that Mayor Walsh did not have a Chief of Staff and asked Daniel if he would be interested in the position. Daniel sent his resume to Mitch, who forwarded it on to the Mayor, but he did not hear back for several weeks. As more time passed and the holiday season approached, he thought to email the Mayor to follow up. To his pleasant surprise, Mayor Walsh got back to him and the two decided to connect when Daniel was back in Boston for the holidays.

While talking, the two found they had a lot in common; they even discussed the New England Patriots season during their first meeting. Upon finishing the meeting, Mayor Walsh told Daniel that his decision on the role would not take long, and that he should hear back shortly. At 10:00 pm on January 1, he received a call from Mayor Walsh informing him that he got the job. He had just turned twenty-nine and was now going to be Chief of Staff for the City of Boston. He was ecstatic! The Mayor's inauguration was on January 6, and Daniel knew it was important for him to be there. Daniel and Mayor Walsh walked into City Hall together, both for the first time in their respective positions. Daniel was new to the role, new to the administration, and dedicated to learning the ins and outs of his new job as quickly as possible to make an impact.

Daniel has learned a lot since first walking into Boston City Hall, but recognizes that he needs to continue to develop. His connection with both the Mayor and the City of Boston have grown immensely. He explains, "The notion of using all that I have learned thus far to help improve the city I was born in means everything to me." Daniel's mindset to never settle and his determination to find what made him the happiest allowed him to try out many of his passions, and ultimately allowed him find the one he liked the best. Daniel knew the value of making connections from a young age and leveraged his network to jump-start his career.

If you could go back in time and tell the eighteen-year-old version of yourself one piece of advice for college, what would it be?

My first piece of advice would be to chill out. Know that just because your family members or friends had a certain career path, that might not be what aligns best to you. I believe that everyone has a lot of passions. You have to be willing to explore life in those areas to know if it is really for you. Enjoy the uncertainty. Enjoy the fact that you are at an age where you can take a risk on a type of career and not have to commit to it. Make sure you exercise all of your interests before you decide on one. Go on the buffet line and try a few different things. Take advantage of all summer internship opportunities and other relevant ways to get experience. Even if you want to be General Manager of the Red Sox, you can still get a taste of what that is like by being a ticketing intern. Don't focus as much on how exactly the first step is supposed to lead to the second step. By virtue of the failures you will go through as part of that journey, you will find yourself in opportunities you never knew were possible. That is the exciting part. Fall into what you love by trying all the things that excite you. Lastly, always take the opportunity to make a connection with someone else because you don't know what the future holds. Every connection you make is an opportunity. You don't know who is going to help you down the line.

—॥॥—

Tara Chang & Katrina Melesciuc
Cofounders of Women's iLab

Growing up, Tara and Katrina were both influenced by strong female mentors who inspired them to think that nothing was outside the realm of possibility. Through their own personal career successes, they were driven to empower and inspire the next generation of female leaders. Tara and Katrina are the cofounders of Women's iLab, an online platform and network to connect women with one another to share their ideas and perspectives. The platform addresses gender equality in the workplace. Tara and Katrina both knew how important making connections had been for their own career success, and wanted to create a platform for other women to connect, learn from one another, and get inspired.

Katrina Melesciuc always enjoyed making connections and getting involved with different groups and organizations. She grew up just north of Boston in the small suburban town of Reading, Massachusetts. Although Katrina was involved in many activities throughout high school, nothing truly stood out as a passion for her as a long-term career. She was unclear on what was next for her future, and worried that this would be a big challenge for her in the college application process. Her dad thought Katrina might like architecture so she started applying to schools with that major. Katrina was shocked and disappointed when she did not get into any of her top choice schools. Fortunately, she had also applied to the University of New Hampshire (UNH) and was accepted. After recovering from the unanticipated rejection of not getting into architecture school, Katrina weighed her options, and decided to attend UNH.

During her freshman year of college, she roomed with her high school friend and decided to start her studies at the Whittemore School of Business. Despite enjoying UNH her freshman year, Katrina still felt conflicted and was unsure of what she truly wanted to get out of her college experience. In order to figure it out, she decided to get involved in a variety of clubs as she had in high school. She joined a sorority (Alpha Phi), started actively making connections on campus, joined student business groups, and became involved with a program called *HerCampus.*

HerCampus is an online magazine featuring articles on gossip, lifestyle, and culture. Originally founded by three women from Harvard, the magazine quickly opened a chapter at Boston University (BU) and other schools around Boston and continues to boast material written by college women for college women. A good friend brought the idea of *HerCampus* to Katrina and she liked the idea of building the first chapter of *HerCampus* at UNH, finding it similar to running her own small business. It seemed like a great opportunity to use her skills and creativity while also getting involved in something new that would challenge her.

Katrina and a small group of friends opened the first *HerCampus* chapter at UNH in 2010, recruited writers, and held monthly meetings. She loved how the magazine brought together women from across the campus for a common purpose. Through *HerCampus*, her sorority, and her various networking groups, Katrina gleaned an acute understanding of people with diverse lifestyles, backgrounds, and ambitions. She liked having unique groups of friends in different settings, and she began to realize that surrounding herself with different people and perspectives was the best thing she could do to learn about herself and build her network.

She realized that by building trusting relationships far and wide, she had developed multiple community circles and was able to excel at UNH. More and more people began to see and understand Katrina's strengths and were quick to point her in the right direction. By building connections and friendships, Katrina grew to better understand herself and her strengths. Through this self-reflection, she declared Business and Accounting as her major, not only because she excelled in the coursework, but because she knew it was a promising career track.

When graduation rolled around in 2011, Katrina was one of the top students in her class and started applying for accounting jobs. Only smaller accounting firms in New Hampshire extended her offers, which did not excite her as she was targeting the Big Four accounting firms. She realized that she needed to better market herself and build connections, just as she had done to set herself up for success at UNH.

Katrina knew that she needed 150 college credits in order to sit for the Certified Public Accountant (CPA) exams, so she decided to start her graduate degree immediately after college at Northeastern University. Upon graduation, she was able to secure a full-time offer at one of the Big Four firms. Wanting to make the most of her summer, she decided to look for an internship opportunity to see what else was out there. Her friend found an opportunity for her at an up-and-coming digital advertising start-up in Boston. Upon being hired, she quickly learned that she loved the culture of the company. The people were young, the office had energy, and all the employees truly cared about the success of the company.

During the internship, she proved herself by working hard and, of course, by making connections. She would often ask people from different departments to grab coffee so she could learn more about the type of work that they did. She met with various people from business development, analytics, marketing, and even met with the CEO. Building these relationships gave her a good sense of what else was out there besides finance and accounting. She also gained invaluable mentors and advocates within the company who wanted to see her succeed. Her exposure to different career paths invited her to reflect on whether finance and accounting was going to make her happy. At the end of the internship, the digital marketing company offered Katrina a full-time job. She loved the company, and they even matched her Big Four salary which was a testament to her work ethic and willingness to make connections during her internship.

Knowing she wanted to try something else besides finance and accounting, she clearly communicated her goals and asked if there would be an opportunity to do so. Thanks to the relationships she built during her internship—she received an offer to join the business strategy team, where she would be working directly for the company's founder and CEO, who was also a serial entrepreneur. Katrina was ecstatic! She kindly informed the Big Four firm that extended her an offer that she would not be starting with them come September.

Working for the company for over a year gave Katrina broad exposure to other departments and she developed an interest in trying something new again and being more client-facing. Taking a leap of faith, Katrina emailed an acquaintance, the Chief Strategy and Analytics Officer, Seraj Bharwani, who had over thirty years of experience in the field building relationships with brand marketers and advertising leaders. She told him that she was very interested in his work and was looking to continue developing in her career by taking on new challenges. He told her that he was impressed with her initiative in reaching out to him and would be happy to hire her onto his team.

Katrina started on the Strategy and Analytics team and worked there for three years. Starting as a junior resource, she worked her way up the ladder to Manager and then Director of Strategic Partnerships where she consulted and advised leading brand marketers on their digital advertising initiatives and strategies. She built multimillion-dollar programs for national brands to help connect with consumers online and enable their brands to become part of the online conversation. The transition into the Strategy and Analytics team was the end result of conveying her goals to one of her connections.

During this time, Katrina built a strong connection with a colleague named Tara Chang, who was Director of Sales for the company. A few years older, Tara became one of her closest friends and mentors. Throughout Katrina's transition onto the Strategy and Analytics team, Tara helped her navigate the gray areas and was instrumental in her success at the company.

Tara Chang grew up in Los Angeles, California, in a Chinese-American family. She attended Marlborough School, an all-girls private high school in

LA, to ensure she had the best education possible. Academically, Tara always loved learning and had a very curious mind. In particular, Tara thrived in her math and science classes. Following in her brother's footsteps, Tara spent countless hours practicing her craft on her high school fencing team, and ultimately became a Junior Olympic fencer. Remember the Disney movie *The Parent Trap?* Tara was Lindsay Lohan's stunt double in the fencing scene! In school, Tara became involved in photography and studied under Mary Ellen Mark, a well-known American photographer. Photography allowed Tara to exercise her creative and artistic side. She even had one of her pictures featured in the Cincinnati Art Institute Museum.

During junior year of high school, Tara's school held a writing competition for the Guerin Scholars Award. The Guerin family had started a program encouraging students to submit an essay about someone they admired and would like to meet someday. Tara wrote her essay about Andrea Jung, the first female CEO and Chairwoman of Avon Products, Inc. Tara won the competition and was awarded the Guerin Scholars Award, and an opportunity to meet Ms. Jung. During the meeting, Tara had the courage to convey her goals and tell Andrea that she would love to intern at Avon if there was an opportunity to do so. To Tara's surprise, Andrea replied that she had the perfect role for her in one of Avon's emerging brands for teens, *Mark.* Tara moved to New York City for the summer and fell in love with both the city and Avon by making a key connection.

Upon returning to LA after the internship, Tara entered her senior year of high school and began thinking ahead to college. Since she had always loved math and science, she decided that she wanted to pursue engineering or a similar career. Massachusetts Institute of Technology (MIT) was her top choice because she was inspired by her father and older brother, both MIT alums. Fortunately, she was accepted into MIT's Sloan School of Management undergraduate program and could not wait to begin the next chapter of her life in Boston.

Upon arriving at MIT, Tara felt like she was in her element. She enjoyed her classes and professors and loved being able to explore her interests on campus through clubs, associations, and other activities. She interned at the New

York Stock Exchange for a summer to gain experience, and back on campus she became involved with the Goldman Sachs trading competition. She was juggling all of these activities in order to find her professional passion. In addition to finance, she also began to explore the marketing industry. She started taking additional marketing classes as part of her degree program and began doing research in MIT's Media Lab to explore her creative side.

Tara decided to major in Management Science, focusing on Marketing, with a minor in Comparative Media Studies. Tara looked into marketing internships to build her resume and get more diverse experience. Through her MIT network, she got in touch with a marketing professional at WebMD. He seemed passionate about his career working in the strategic partnership division, and when Tara expressed her interest in gaining experience in that field, he helped her secure a summer internship. Tara used her college network to get her to the next step in her career. That summer, she interned at WebMD in New York City and loved the experience; ultimately culminating in a full-time offer to work in their Marketing and Sales group.

While she enjoyed the work at WebMD and excelled at her job, something was missing. She had been working in a big corporate environment and wanted to be involved in building something new in order to see the direct impact of her work. At the time, Tara's brother had a contact at a digital advertising analytics start-up in Boston, and thought that a fast-paced start-up environment would be the perfect fit for her. She connected with the founders of the company and discovered they had also attended MIT's Sloan School of Management. Tara interviewed and got the job.

At twenty-two, Tara moved back to Boston from New York City and started as a Business Analyst working for the Chief Strategy and Analytics Officer, Seraj Bharwani. Coincidentally, Seraj would later help Katrina switch departments to come work for him. He trained Tara and Katrina and both women consider him a member of their personal board. When Tara started, the company was a small start-up with only twenty to thirty employees. This was exactly the type of company and environment she had been seeking. Due to the rapid growth of the company, they needed to expand to New York City and Tara was asked to help build out the new office and take on more of a sales role. At the time, she barely knew what sales consisted of, but she was ready for a new challenge.

This was the first sales office the company had, and since then they have expanded to four offices across the United States. The company's rapid growth continued and in 2012, Tara also helped the Chief Strategy and Analytics Officer expand the company's client base internationally into Canada. Tara continued to grow with the company and was eventually promoted to Vice President of Sales and Account Management. She is now completing a one-year accelerated MBA program at Northwestern's Kellogg School of Management. True to her nature, she is currently her class' Marketing Director for the Women's Business Association and Co-President of the Kellogg Entrepreneur's Organization.

While working together at the digital marketing company, Tara and Katrina frequently traveled together for work, attending different events, meeting new people, and building relationships. One night after a conference, Tara and Katrina discussed their desire to have more female leaders in their lives to admire and emulate. They talked about addressing the problem and created a website for women to connect and share ideas and advice by writing articles and sharing content. It was that night that Women's iLab was born. Within three months, Tara and Katrina built the website, set up social media sites, and recruited several women to start writing articles to help spread the word. Once the name, website, and social media sites were established, they started writing articles and connecting with other women. They did not do any advertising for the website and only marketed it through word of mouth. They quickly found out that people loved their mission and noticed increased traffic to the site as people started to spread the word.

Their success was also fueled by several strategic relationships. Tara and Katrina agreed to meet one new person each week to learn about their story and tell them about Women's iLab. They knew that by expanding their network and making intentional new connections, they could share and spread the Women's iLab mission. Through the process, they reached out to Daniel Koh. Katrina's uncle worked at the state house and suggested they talk to Daniel because he too, was impressive, young, and successful. Tara and Katrina met with Daniel in the summer of 2014 and told him all about Women's iLab and the mission they hoped to achieve. He loved the idea and introduced them to a group called ONEin3 that addresses the needs of more than one-third of Boston community members between the ages of twenty and thirty-four. Soon after, Women's iLab became a finalist for the ONEin3 Impact Award, an annual award that the City of Boston and Mayor Marty Walsh select for upcoming companies and/or organizations that are making a civic impact in the City of Boston. As further testament to the brand's growing success, Women's iLab was a top four finalist among other social impact start-ups.

From there, Katrina was invited to be a participant on a ONEin3 networking panel in Boston, for which the Vice President and Program Director of the Startup Institute was the moderator. This led to a connection with the President of the Startup Institute who has been an amazing connector for Tara and Katrina, introducing them to the former Chief Operating Officer of the PayPal Media Network who is now a mentor. Katrina also built a strong relationship with one of the other panelists who was a CEO and founder of several companies. Katrina now joins his monthly entrepreneur dinners with new and established entrepreneurs based in Boston; a testament to the power of connection in action.

Another strategic partnership that this powerhouse duo formed through Daniel Koh was with the start-up accelerator, MassChallenge. Tara and Katrina had always believed that there were not enough female entrepreneurs and saw MassChallenge as an opportunity to change this. Women's iLab partnered with MassChallenge to drive more female engagement and awareness of the organization. Tara and Katrina helped MassChallenge recruit more female resources, speakers, and more women to submit applications describing their ideas and companies to the MassChallenge competition. In return, MassChallenge helped spotlight Women's iLab at different events in Boston. That year, MassChallenge received the most female-led company applications it had ever received and over 40% of the start-ups in the final accelerator had a female founder.

Tara and Katrina also became involved with their longtime advocate, the Boston Chamber of Commerce. Women's iLab was selected as the first

Inaugural Innovation Spotlight at the January 2015 Women's Network breakfast to speak in front of over 200 women as the voice of Boston's start-up industry. Women's iLab was also selected to join the Chamber as a start-up organization member and became involved with the mentor-matching program. They were fortunately matched with an extremely talented and well-networked woman who was the former president of Digitas Boston and currently is the Chief Marketing Officer (CMO) of a real estate platform called Altisource. To this day, she advises them on the digital presence of Women's iLab and their career development. In return, Tara and Katrina share new ideas and perspectives from the millennial audience and start-up industry to ensure the relationship is mutually beneficial.

Since Women's iLab first formed, it has been hugely successful. In its first year, the organization touched readers in 135 countries. The experience with Women's iLab also allowed Tara and Katrina to solidify their personal career missions. This venture was their outlet to make a tangible impact on the world and create a movement to showcase women leaders across the world. Both Tara and Katrina found something that they love doing and are passionate about. They were successful in their own right before creating Women's iLab, but now, they are making an impact on the lives of other women around the world.

If you could go back in time and tell the eighteen-year-old version of yourself one piece of advice for college, what would it be?

Tara—I have learned a great deal through my experiences and accomplishments. Reflecting upon my career development, relationships, both personal and professional, my advice would be – take time to maintain. Sometimes it only takes five minutes to strengthen a relationship. It is important to regularly invest and maintain those relationships that you build with classmates, professors, and industry contacts as those people are very likely to contribute to your professional development in some way in the future. Strong relationships will have a significant impact on your life and they are cultivated over time. Even now, I continue to remind myself to send notes to mentors [who] I have had in the past to maintain those relationships. I realize now how much my career has been influenced by the many people I have met throughout my career. When you are busy, it is easy to get caught up with your daily activities; you never know when someone might be that person that will help connect you to your dream job.

Katrina—Building relationships and a network is not about thinking about what you can get out of people, but rather what you can give. The best relationships formed (both business and personally) are those that are mutually supportive of one another. As you are meeting new people and building new connections, keep an open mind. As you are growing and changing, your friendships should be as well. Your personal brand is not defined by one singular thing, but rather the puzzle of passions and experiences that you create for yourself. You should create different community circles that tap into each of these different puzzle pieces and grow them by thinking about what you can bring into the circle. You have unique strengths and capabilities, that others in those circles may be lacking and vice versa. I have even seen that my mentors, who have been CEOs and CMOs of companies, still come to me looking for advice or ideas because I can bring a unique perspective that they may be lacking. Approach your relationships and circles thinking about what you can give, and then you will get wonderful things out of them.

—ᨑ—

Remy Carpinito
Founder & CEO, CampusTap

Remy Carpinito is the Founder and CEO of CampusTap, a leading career and mentoring platform that helps students and alumni make meaningful connections and launch successful careers. A finalist in BostInno's 2015 "50 on Fire" year-end awards celebration, he was recognized as one of Boston's top inventors, disrupters, luminaries, and newsmakers across all industries. However, as we will learn, Remy's hometown success in Boston started many years prior, just twenty minutes north of the city.

As a college student, you constantly meet new people. Your social circles rapidly expand as you begin new courses, join clubs, play sports, complete internships, and attend parties. It is important to keep your eyes open as your network grows. Remember, there is no such thing as a "bad connection"; any connection can open the doors to big opportunities. This is because these people typically have social networks that are much different than your own. Like

Tara and Katrina, Remy recognized an opportunity to make people's lives better, and his vision became a reality on college campuses, thanks to the support and financial aid of his social circle. He knew how to activate his connections and was not afraid to let people know what he needed. By leveraging his connections efficiently, he was able to catapult CampusTap to where it is today.

Remy grew up in Reading, Massachusetts, just north of Boston. While growing up, baseball and hockey consumed the majority of his time and attention. After carefully weighing his options for college, he decided to attend Suffolk University for his undergraduate degree. Being able to play baseball, live in Boston, and be close to family were ideal options for him at the time.

His connection to the baseball team helped him integrate into college quickly as he immediately had thirty or so friends on the team. In college, he also pursued his passion for technology and combined it with his entrepreneurial thinking to start his own company, RemTech Consulting. Living in the dorms, he realized a problem—new incoming students didn't know how to hook up any of their TVs, computers, or printers. Remy immediately started putting up flyers around campus with tear-off business cards at the bottom. Almost immediately, his phone was ringing off the hook. During winter break, he was also able to find an internship doing network consulting to continue to test his interest in technology. The one-month internship ended up extending far beyond winter break and gave him valuable IT experience which confirmed his interest in that type of career.

That summer after freshman year, Remy knew that a new sports complex in North Reading, MA was opening, so he answered a formal bid for the IT work and got it. He quickly hired his roommate and started wiring the entire building, mounting all the TVs, and setting up the computers as well as a small server. That one job alone paid for his living expenses for that entire summer and for most of his junior year.

Having worked all summer, he took some time to think about his future. He decided to make the very hard decision to quit baseball that fall to further pursue his interest in technology. With more time on his hands, he got a security job at Battery Wharf, a luxury residence on the waterfront in Boston's

North End. The job afforded him ample time to do his coursework and read up on the latest technology trends during his shifts.

Remy also wanted to get ahead academically and talked to his professors who suggested that he join a club. He joined the Information Systems (IS) club and attended an event hosted by Fidelity recruiters. Fidelity, a large investment management company, was offering IT internships to select students for the following summer. Through the event, Remy made a connection with the recruiters, submitted an application, and was one of two students to secure a full-time internship for that coming summer as a data analyst.

That semester, Remy decided to make a prototype of a smartphone application he saw a need for. His idea was to make it easier for college students to find clubs and events on and off campus. He had remembered his experience of ripping business cards off flyers to find the IS club and knew there was a better way to share this information. This was the beginning of CampusTap.

Before leaving his job at Battery Wharf later that year, he caught wind that a seasoned software director was living on the property. Remy's security manager encouraged him to talk to him. He finally connected with him and pitched his idea. The software director liked the application and told Remy he had a little free time and might be able to help. He connected Remy to his friend and past colleague, AJ in San Francisco, who had recently left a technology company that had been recently acquired. After connecting over Skype, AJ and Remy decided to develop the application together.

After junior year, Remy started his internship at Fidelity and worked there for the entire summer. In addition to working at Fidelity, he was also continuing to build the prototype of the CampusTap app with AJ. Once the prototype was completed, he went around to several colleges in Boston to get feedback on the idea. The feedback he got was that it was a cool idea but that it needed to be more substantial. Although this was disappointing to hear, Remy took the constructive feedback and put it to work. After thinking about how to expand his idea, Remy and AJ contemplated building a private social platform. They saw an opportunity to make something better and expand the scope of CampusTap.

Prior to returning to school for his senior year, Fidelity extended Remy a generous full-time offer. Before committing, he wanted to see what would happen with CampusTap. Remy and AJ soon learned that they needed capital to continue developing the platform, so Remy started leveraging his network and asked friends and family if they wanted to invest. One of his uncles was the first to come to the table and gave him his first check for CampusTap. It was enough money for him to feel comfortable turning down his offer at Fidelity to stay focused on his vision. His plan was to move out to San Francisco to work with AJ. They had been working together for over a year at that point and had never met face-to-face.

Remy knew he was going to need more capital, so during the spring semester of his senior year, he applied to Suffolk University's Product Innovation competition, even though he knew hundreds of students would also be submitting business plans to win capital and free professional services. He won the competition and received $4,000 in cash and $9,000 in services for CampusTap which bought him some more time.

After graduating, he moved out to San Francisco to work on CampusTap full time with AJ. The business was running all summer on the capital he had received from his uncle and the product innovation competition, which was quickly running out. He also brought on another developer to speed up the work. By August, the business again needed to raise more capital. On a trip back to Boston that September, Remy called up his former security boss from Battery Wharf, who had always wanted to invest. Sure enough, he did. He also got some more friends and family to invest. He now had a little more breathing room, and a few more months of runway to continue developing the platform. Remy had come back to Boston that September with a fully functional prototype which he wanted to start testing. He set up a small user group that fall at Suffolk University with approximately 100 users to get real-time feedback from students.

The capital he had raised ended up lasting until February of that following year. At that time, he had just been accepted to MassChallenge in hopes of winning additional funding for his business. In round two of the

MassChallenge competition later that spring, he had to pitch CampusTap to a room of judges. One of the judges worked at the MIT entrepreneurship center and introduced himself to Remy after his pitch. He was interested in the platform and exchanged contact information. Remy knew he did well during the pitch that day and called AJ immediately after in excitement to tell him that he thought they were on to the final round, and that they got someone's business card from MIT. Two weeks after round two judging, he received word that CampusTap was selected as a MassChallenge 2014 finalist with access to office space, mentors, and unlimited professional services.

Not long after, Remy connected with the judge from MIT who put him in touch with a professor that was looking for a platform similar to CampusTap. MIT was looking to leverage the platform to connect students with projects sponsored by various companies and organizations. He ended up meeting with the professor and demonstrating CampusTap's capabilities. She was excited and told him that some things would need to be customized, but that they were in. He had finally sold the CampusTap platform to his first school, and not just any school, but MIT!

During MassChallenge, Remy heard of an opportunity to partake in "Mull-mersion Day," sponsored by Mullen, one of the most elite and innovative marketing organizations in the world. Remy applied and was accepted to receive feedback on the CampusTap product from their experts. The social media manager from Mullen ended up being a Wheaton College alumnus and talked to him about the problems she had reconnecting with the school. In the fall of 2014, she put him in touch with the Director of Career Services at Wheaton College to talk about CampusTap. Within several weeks, Remy had pitched and secured a deal with them.

After closing Wheaton, he ran into a close contact at a networking event for start-ups in Boston that Constant Contact was sponsoring. By rekindling an old connection, he learned that Constant Contact was accepting applications for a new start-up accelerator program called the SMB

Innoloft. The company had created a modern space for start-ups to work at their office in Waltham, MA, where they provided both funding and resources. He ended up applying after talking to his team about the opportunity and CampusTap was accepted to pitch their business. Remy went into Constant Contact and gave a great presentation. Three hours later, he got a call that they had been accepted into the program. His team was given office space, a $10,000 marketing budget, access to the Constant Contact team, and the opportunity to connect with their Higher Education partners. Over the summer of 2015, the team focused all of their sales and marketing efforts on expanding beyond Boston and refining the career services components of the CampusTap platform. They attended several national career services and alumni-related conferences and started building momentum.

Just before the Constant Contact accelerator started, the team secured a final meeting with Bentley University. It was a testament to the team's persistence as they had reached out to Bentley earlier in the year to build the relationship. Remy had met with the Director of Career Services at one of the major conferences that summer and she was an advocate for innovation and technology in the career services space. She loved the platform and wanted to hold a bigger demonstration at Bentley to show others. The CampusTap team went to Bentley for the larger demo and a few weeks later, signed a deal. The University, which is ranked as one of the top business schools in the country, was a huge win for CampusTap. During that summer, the CampusTap team also landed Skidmore and Santa Monica College as clients and was excited about what was next.

At twenty-four, Remy was running full-steam ahead, following his passion for technology and entrepreneurship. There had been many ups and downs along the way, but Remy knew where he was heading. He had built a great business model and others were now starting to pay attention. By leveraging his connections and meeting new people along the way, Remy was able to accelerate the process of making CampusTap a success.

If you could go back in time and tell the eighteen-year-old version of yourself one piece of advice for college, what would it be?

Accept the uncertainties, don't be afraid to fail, and take as many opportunities as you can. You don't have to have everything figured out; the beauty of college is the opportunity to explore what you like and what you're good at. Lean on the people around you whether it be professors, peers, alumni, or individuals you meet at networking events, for advice and support. They've been in your shoes and have valuable experiences and advice to share.

—⁓—

Connecting The Dots

Daniel, Tara, Katrina, and Remy all leveraged the power of human connection to build their support system of mentors, partners, advocates, and cheerleaders. Through their dedication to developing and maintaining these relationships, their connections in return provided them with opportunities that opened doors. Reflect on how they made their connections and leverage their advice to map out a plan of action for how you can start building your support system to find the next step in your career. You can use the following tools and concepts to get started.

(1) **Master Your Elevator Speech:** Picture for a minute that you just got into an elevator headed up to your internship or part-time job. It's early, you haven't had coffee yet, and the CEO of the company steps into the elevator just before the doors close and makes eye contact with you. You know who she is because you have seen her on the company's website and once before in the lobby. It is just you two in the elevator as the doors close. You smile to acknowledge her, but you have your headphones on and could potentially back out of saying something. What do you do? Most elevator pitch stories we learn about in college sound like the story above. An elevator pitch doesn't need to make you feel like you are going to crap your pants in the elevator saying "Hi" to the CEO. You are simply introducing yourself

to one of the other seven billion people on this planet. Introducing yourself does not need to be an awkward encounter. Have the courage and confidence to say "Hello" and make it known that you exist. Start practicing your elevator speech in a variety of situations such as on campus, at the gym, and while shopping. The only way you will get comfortable with this seemingly awkward situation is if you practice. With everyone. Pretend that everyone is that CEO. Who knows, maybe that "practice conversation" ends up being someone who truly is important for your career.

(2) **Clubs, Organizations, and Campus Events:** Daniel, Tara, Katrina, and Remy were all involved with different clubs and organizations on campus which allowed them to broaden their network and build strong beneficial relationships. As we mentioned in Chapter 2 about drawing on a blank sheet of paper, work with career services and other departments to get an inventory of all the clubs, organizations, and honors programs your college offers. These programs are great ways to not only meet new students, but also greet and get to know professionals through networking events, panels, and guest speakers.

(3) **Events and Conferences:** Colleges hold many different events on campus that students can tap into. Career panels, guest talks, and networking events with employers are great opportunities to learn something new and make connections. Work with career services and other departments at your school to stay on top of all the upcoming events each semester. Identify which events you want to go to that align with your interests, fit them into your schedule, and commit to going. Don't back out because you are tired or "busy". Make it important and work your day around these events. There are also many events and conferences available to students outside of their colleges. Websites like Eventbrite make it easy for students to find events and conferences in their area that they may be interested in. See if you can find a friend with similar interests to go with you to these events so that you can work as a team to make connections. It also helps to do some research in advance. Look up the format of the event or conference, make note of who will be presenting and what topics will be

discussed to maximize your time and potential investment. Not all events and conferences are free, but be resourceful and see if your college could sponsor you or if there is a way to get a student discount.

(4) **Alumni Network:** Tap into your college's alumni network and reach out to alumni who are in careers you are interested in to make a connection and learn about what they do. Typically, career services departments will have a database of alumni that students can search through or an application like CampusTap. Once you identify some connections you want to reach out to, send them an introductory email and inquire about connecting via phone or in person so you can learn about his or her career. People love talking about their stories and most alumni are willing to help out a college student from their alma mater.

(5) **Professors:** Make connections with the professors who teach classes that interest and intrigue you. Typically, professors also have professional experience in the field they are teaching in, and many times still have a diverse network of people they could potentially connect you with. Tell your professors about your goals and the types of careers you are trying to explore; they may be able to help.

(6) **Social Media:** As we will learn more about in the next chapter on creating your story, social media platforms like LinkedIn and Facebook can also help you make connections. You can use these platforms to search for professionals who are working in a specific career or for an employer that interests you. Send them a message, introduce yourself and inquire about connecting to learn about their career.

Today, through the use of social media, our communities extend much farther than our day-to-day interactions. Thanks to these platforms, you can connect to friends, family, potential employers or employees, and inspiring mentors from all around the world. Our access to our close connections and everyone else is now a thousand times greater. Use the tools that are at your disposal to connect with different people and build your network and support system for success.

Making connections with others and bridging multiple networks opens the door to finding new and different career opportunities that can help maximize your return on your college investment. Get out there and start meeting the right people who can be catalysts for your career.

CHAPTER 4
Creating Your Story

"Your brand is what people say about you
when you're not in the room."[27]
- JEFF BEZOS, FOUNDER OF AMAZON

Most people go through life reacting to situations in which they find themselves. These are the people who, down the road, wind up looking back on life with regret. They blame others for missed opportunities and failures that occurred along the way. The reality is, if you're not taking control of your life and are leaving things to chance, you are gambling with your greatest asset: time. If you set out to make something of your future, then be that person: breathe, eat, and live like that person you see in your mind. We all have unique stories that differentiate us based on our backgrounds and the paths we have taken in life. Your past will never change; however, your differentiators and life experiences will continue to be powerful tools for your career moving forward. It is up to you to intentionally use those experiences to understand who you are, what you do best, and how to develop into the best version of yourself. You are in charge of creating your story and your brand as an individual. What do you want to say?

If someone were to ask you when you turned fifty years old, "What do you want to be remembered for?" What would your response be? It is ok if you don't have the answer right off the bat. Very few individuals can clearly answer these type of questions fully without time to reflect. However, when you think about the future, your values, and what you want to be known for, you begin to see flashes of your future. The flashes show you the personal brand you wish to emulate. Understanding your personal brand helps you set yourself up to create a story that empowers you and differentiates you in a world that will soon be filled with 262 million college students competing for different careers.[28]

Over time, you will be able to frame an answer as to what you want to be remembered for; then you will be able to backtrack and create a personal roadmap that will enable you to maximize your time and investment in college. Grab onto the steering wheel of life, discover your interests, plan ahead, and make intentional choices. Each and every day, as you draw on a blank sheet of paper and make connections, your brand will communicate to others what your story is, and more importantly, where it is going.

Branding is about creating experiences that foster lasting memories and influence the decisions we make. Google, Apple, Starbucks, Nike, and BMW are all ubiquitous brands. Are there memories or emotions that come to mind when you read the names of these companies? Think, for instance, about the last time you walked into a Starbucks. What did you experience? Starbucks tries to offer its customers more than just a cup of coffee. Everything from their lounge areas, to free Wi-Fi, to custom drink orders, to the baristas writing your name on your cup expresses familiarity and makes you feel welcome. Starbucks intentionally differentiates itself by being a place where customers can do work, meet a friend, or just hang out and enjoy a cup of freshly brewed coffee and the morning news-paper. This experience and branding is premeditated and has helped catapult Starbucks to global success. The most successful companies in the world under-stand the value of a powerful brand and develop theirs by exceeding customer expectations and being trendsetters within their respective industries.

Understanding what makes brands of successful companies so influential is a good starting point for defining your own personal brand. Consider yourself as the CEO of your career and start defining how you want to communicate your brand to others. Your personal brand is the impression taken away from the total experience someone has when interacting with you. Similar to what was de-scribed above, what experiences and memories do you leave someone with? Your personal brand is driven from your core values. It also spans from your nonverbal communication (facial expressions, gestures, eye contact, and body language), to the things you say and how you say them. Your personal brand allows others to get to know who you are as a person but is also a way for you get to know a lot more about yourself too. While it is important to think about how you want to develop your personal brand, it is just as important to first understand what your brand is today. Take a moment to ask yourself, *What am I known for?*

A national survey focused on human capital indicated that "[l]ess than 15% of people have truly defined their personal brand and less than 5% are living it consistently at work each and every day."[29] Let's work on closing this gap. The important thing to know about your personal brand is that while you may define it – others perceive it. Periodically, ask others for feedback on your personal development to understand what they think you bring to the table. Leverage those perceptions to make small changes as needed that will outwardly reflect the brand that you want to convey.

Influential leaders like the late Steve Jobs, Richard Branson, and Beyoncé —all bring their unique personalities and backstories to the forefront of their organizations. In most cases, their personal brand actually helps define and make up what the brand of their organization ends up becoming. The key takeaway is to be yourself. Define what makes you unique, understand your strengths and weaknesses, and use them to help inform your personal brand as you develop into the best version of yourself.

Bringing your brand to life also extends beyond the classroom and into the world of social media. Just like with the decisions you make every day in your interactions with others and yourself, your personal brand is evidenced in your posts on Facebook, LinkedIn, Twitter, Instagram, etc. Ensure your brand grows and strengthens the right way across all your forums of communication. Yes, this does seem like a major commitment on your part, but your future is worth the investment. How would a stranger define your personal brand after looking at your social media pages? Is there a point of disconnect between how you show up in-person and online? Think about how Dwayne "The Rock" Johnson or Kevin Hart are promoting their brands on social media. Do a quick search for their social media profiles and see how they are creating their story using these social media platforms. Your personal brand is your gateway to differentiating yourself in a crowd of many, use all the tools and resources available to you to stand out.

As you try new and different things to test your interests and make connections with the right individuals, your story will evolve and impact your personal brand and identity. Take a leadership stance, know your vision, and create a story that will be a page-turner for life.

The next section of this chapter will introduce you to the final three remarkable interviewees. Even though their visions were still being developed, from childhood through college, they consistently communicated their brand and created their own roadmap to obtain a career that empowers them. In reading through their stories, think about how they aligned their vision to their careers and developed their personal brand to support their journey.

—〰—

Daquan Oliver
Cofounder & CEO of Jossle and Founder
& Executive Director of WeThrive

Creating your own story is a lifelong journey that is inspired by self-motivation and your will to succeed. Small chapters of your story begin and end each day with the decisions you make. It is never too early to start creating your story. Daquan Oliver, an innovator and entrepreneur, began his journey at the young age of seven. He made intentional decisions throughout high school and college and set goals for himself to be the best student to ever graduate from Babson College. Through his hard work, he is now working full time on the two very successful ventures he started while in college. He is also the recipient of several people-to-watch honors, including recognition from the Clinton Foundation as one of five Black Student Leaders to Watch in 2014. During a TEDx Talk in November 2014, he also shared some mind-provoking thoughts on the "Power of Chaos." Through experimenting with his interests, Daquan found what he was passionate about and positioned himself for a career that allowed him to make an impact on his community in his own unique way.

You may be familiar with the adage "Your reputation precedes you." More than ever it's true that one's reputation will be shared and prejudged before a face-to-face interaction. After all, the same social media platforms that can be used to tap into new connections can also promote public and permanent defamation. Now is the time to maximize the tools around you, such as social media, and make them work for you, not against you. Take a moment to review your latest Instagram pictures and Facebook posts. Do you look and sound intelligent? Is your productivity evidenced? What about your interests? At this moment, can any one of your social platforms launch you into the atmosphere of post-graduate success? No? Don't worry. It's not too late to transform your social media platforms to reflect your brand. When we were writing this book, we took a moment to look at Daquan's Facebook page. Right away, you will notice Daquan's cover photo, a picture of what we can assume is a close reading of Osho's *Yoga: The Birth of Being.*

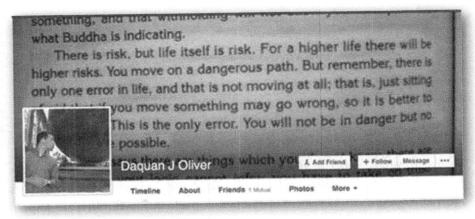

You can already deduce one of Daquan's most inspiring personal brand attributes: risk taker. Continue perusing Daquan's public profile, and you will notice that, since his arrival at Babson College, he has used Facebook to build beneficial connections and promote social awareness about interesting topics, such as the social inequality of public schools and the perseverance and sacrifice of single mothers.

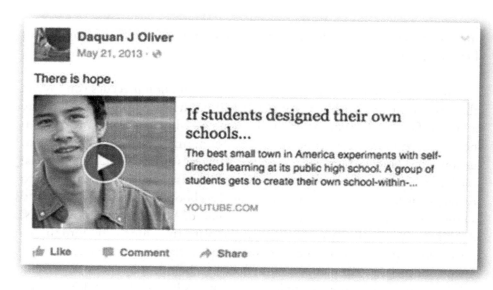

With every public post, his work ethic and passion is evident and inspiring.

In minutes, you can deduce several more characteristics of Daquan's personal brand: demonstrative, ambitious, hands-on, and compassionate. How did he get to this point? Let's take a peek inside the life of Daquan Oliver.

Daquan grew up in both Mount Vernon and New Rochelle, New York. Mount Vernon, a low income neighborhood riddled with high crime rates, had its differences from New Rochelle, a middle class neighborhood offering an array of opportunities to a young man looking to make something of himself. Being part of these two neighborhoods made him realize how a kid's activities can impact his mindset and influence his future endeavors.

Daquan was raised in a single parent environment by his mother, which in turn gave him the opportunity to mature at an early age. He became a man from a young age, dedicated to helping his hard-working mom. One of his defining moments occurred when he was seven years old. He wanted a toy that his mom could not afford. Determined to get this toy, he found a stack of newspapers to sell and came up with the money to buy it. This was the first sign to him that he had the ability to create his own future through his actions and mindset.

In high school, Daquan continued to experiment with business when he started a candy franchise. He would use his Costco membership to buy candy and return to school to sell the candy for a profit. Even at that young of an age, he understood the importance of teamwork and strategically had three other students selling for him to maximize on the opportunity. He was making, on average, about $1,000 a month selling candy. But this did not derail his foremost responsibility. He remained focused on making his own way to help his family through their financial struggles. Daquan bought his own cell phone and paid his own cell phone bills while in high school and did not burden his mom with extra expenses. Through these small acts of responsibility, he learned valuable lessons in independence. This mindset would forever support his entrepreneurial activities and become embedded in his personal brand.

Daquan began to establish a reputation amongst his family members, teachers, and friends as a business-savvy entrepreneur. This label resonated with him going into his junior year of high school. While looking through the college pamphlets that started to come in the mail, he noticed a number of schools, including Babson College, the number one school for entrepreneurship. In his search for the right college, he also made sure to take calculated risks. During his high school career, he was an All-American and one of the top runners in the state of New York. To this day, he holds the record for the mile and 4x800 events at his high school. Daquan made a highlight reel of his high school events and sent it to the track coaches of colleges he applied to in order to maximize his chances of not only getting admitted but potentially earning a scholarship. Babson College, amazed by both his story and his athletic ability, extended an offer of admittance with a full academic scholarship.

Even though Daquan graduated with honors from high school, he arrived on Babson's campus with a feeling of inferiority because he was from a low income background. Some students at Babson had come from affluent backgrounds both in the United States and abroad. However, he gathered the courage to walk up to the President of Babson during his freshman year to introduce himself at an event. He told the President to keep his eyes peeled and informed him that he would be one of the best Babson graduates for years to come. He intentionally set a public goal for himself, which he used as motivation going forward.

From the moment he set foot on campus, he witnessed students enter and graduate Babson with their own established businesses. This gave him the confirmation that he, too, could achieve what his counterparts had. He continued to get involved on campus, and during his freshman year won the annual business plan competition. The competition included MBA students and alumni, and this achievement boosted his confidence and propelled his drive to achieve more.

Although his idea that won the business plan competition did not work out, the entrepreneurial drive within Daquan and his team led to the founding of a marketing agency named Jossle. The idea for Jossle came from Daquan and his cofounders during the weekend before spring finals of his freshman year. They recognized and capitalized on an opportunity to help companies market to college students. Over the course of that weekend, Daquan and the other cofounders completed the initial model for the idea, created a website, and had already attracted hundreds of students to visit the page. By the end of the summer, Jossle had 10,000 students signed up across the nation. With a refined business model, Jossle beat out professional marketing firms and landed Zipcar as one of their first clients.

Jossle is not Daquan's only current venture. His second venture, WeThrive, is a nonprofit that invites college student mentors to teach entrepreneurial skills to low-income middle and high school students. Although founded in his sophomore year, the idea of WeThrive originated when he was fourteen and frustrated thinking he had no future ahead of him. Imagine being fourteen years old and thinking you and your mom were not going to make it out of your financial struggles. Daquan and his mom were challenged to keep up with their home payments and everyday living expenses. He contemplated where the opportunities were for him and his family. Would his future be no different than what he was experiencing? He consistently fought this mindset and made a promise to himself to take matters into his own hands. He promised himself that one day, he would be remembered in his community for being a great entrepreneur and would create a program that would pave the way for underprivileged kids like him with drive and passion to also make something of their lives.

In Daquan's sophomore year at Babson, his vision for WeThrive came to fruition. He learned of Barton Road, a comprehensive after-school tutoring and enrichment program for elementary and middle school children. Once introduced, Daquan knew he was one step closer to the promise he made to himself. Daquan was later elected to lead the program and capitalized on the opportunity to design the entrepreneurial program the way he had envisioned it, giving birth to WeThrive.

From a young age, Daquan knew exactly what he wanted. He set goals for himself and made very intentional decisions to create the career he wanted. He continued to grow Jossle and WeThrive during his junior and senior years at Babson into organizations that would sustain him upon graduation. While his peers were trying to find summer internships that would translate into full-time job offers, Daquan was focused on making his vision of entrepreneurship and owning his own business a reality.

Fast forward to post graduation, Daquan is now running his two organizations full time. The Jossle team recently moved out to Los Angeles from Boston. Jossle was projected to have revenues of $250,000 to $300,000 in

2015. The organization has seven employees who are all part-time for now, and an editor-in-chief for the online magazine who was scheduled to go full-time upon her graduation in May 2015.

WeThrive continues to expand and is currently establishing programs with Wellesley College, Brandeis University, and Boston College. The group also began entrepreneurship lessons through Artistius for Humanity, a Boston nonprofit that exposes inner-city students to the arts. WeThrive recently became the newest Fellow of Echoing Green in June 2015. Echoing Green is an organization responsible for some of the world's most well-known social innovation enterprises such as City Year, Citizen Schools, and Teach for America, to name a few. As an Echoing Green Fellow, Daquan received $80,000 in funding for two years and will participate in leadership development events, receive mentoring from leading business professionals, and become part of a global network of leaders that will all allow him to continue to develop his story and brand.

Daquan was always intrinsically motivated to better himself and the lives of his loved ones. His passion and ability to create a memorable brand allowed him to embrace success early on in his career and be a role model for members of his community. As the Cofounder and CEO of Jossle and the Founder & Executive Director of WeThrive, Daquan's story is only just beginning.

If you could go back in time and tell the eighteen-year-old version of yourself one piece of advice for college, what would it be?

I would say two things: (1) dream bigger and (2) believe in yourself. Going to Babson College, not only taught me to dream even bigger than I already was, but also to have an impeccable belief and confidence that whatever goal I set for myself, I would find a way to make it happen. Your goals will not always be achieved the way you would like, but the most important thing is that your goal is achieved! You must always take advantage of the opportunities presented to you no matter where you are.

—⚘—

Matt Evans
Northeast Area Scout for the Washington Redskins

Matt Evans is a Northeast Area Scout for the Washington Redskins, a National Football League (NFL) team. From a young age, Matt cultivated his career path by chasing his passion for playing football. He always had a determination to succeed and lived life humbly, proving doubters wrong. Through his dedication to his craft of playing football, Matt earned the highest accolade in the nation for his position while playing in college. Both on and off the field, he was creating his story and shaping his personal brand as an athlete and a leader. After graduating college and seeing his chance at a professional football career slip away, he knew he wanted to stay close to the sport. With his love of the game, his high football IQ, and his determination to prove his worth, he landed an internship with the Washington Redskins organization that he turned into a career.

As you develop your personal brand, you should ask for feedback and constructive criticism. If you can learn to embrace failure and perceive it as an opportunity to grow, then you will become a better version of you—the 2.0 version. Too many students fear failure, so they play it safe and do not take risks. This fixed mindset robs many talented individuals of the opportunity to become even greater than they are. Stanford University's Dr. Carol Dweck has conducted research on the fixed and growth mindsets; her work suggests that individuals who take risks and embrace failure as an opportunity to learn from mistakes make better leaders and partners, celebrate more accomplishments, and live happier lives. Matt Evans earned his career success by continuously seeking opportunities to grow and learning from those around him. His determination, work ethic, professionalism, and knowledge of the game he loved never ceased to impress his coaches and teammates.

Matt's story started in his hometown of Hanover, Massachusetts, twenty minutes south of Boston. When high school rolled around, he decided to attend Thayer Academy in Braintree, MA, as most of his family had attended the school, including his dad, brother, and sister. Matt decided on Thayer because they had a really good sports program, especially for football, which was his true passion. During high school, he knew playing football was going to be his number one focus. Even during the summer, he would stay active by training and exercising two and a half hours a day and going to football camps. Each semester, his focus was on training his body to get bigger, stronger, and faster so he could achieve his goal of playing Division I football.

The summer after his sophomore year at Thayer, Division I college football programs started taking an interest in his skills. The realization that people were interested in him as an athlete fueled his motivation. He was grateful that all his hard work up until then had finally paid off. He was slightly small for the linebacker position as he was only about 200 pounds in high school which was an obstacle that he was motivated to overcome. As a smaller linebacker, he knew he would have to do a lot to stand out at camps for Division I football programs. He attended camps at Boston College, UMass Amherst, and the University of Maryland but they all thought he was not big enough to play the linebacker position.

A few Division I AA schools, such as Delaware, Northeastern, UNH, and Brown University extended Matt offers to play football for them. With no Division I A offers on the table, he had narrowed the other choices down to Brown or UNH, and decided to commit to UNH as they were the first school to offer him a full-scholarship and had a more established football program. One of his defining values is loyalty, and he never forgot who took the first chance on him.

After football season and committing to play football at UNH his senior year, he took basketball season off. He wanted to focus the majority of his attention on preparing himself for the next level. During the summer after high school, Matt started pre-season training. One of his biggest obstacles once he got to UNH was actually learning the playbook. It was completely different from anything he'd experienced at the high school level and it took him a long time to learn and feel comfortable with it.

In football, just like in any other sport, to be able to play fast with impact, the playbook needs to become second nature. The problem was that no one was teaching him the playbook during the season as the team's focus was on game preparation for each week. After that season was over and heading into the following spring, UNH got a new linebacker coach. The position coach took Matt under his wing and helped him practice the plays in the playbook. He saw something in him and told the other coaches that Matt was going to be his project in the off-season. He simplified the playbook for Matt so he could see and practice the plays.

For his redshirt freshman year and second season, Matt started off third on the depth chart and it was his goal to be starting at the linebacker position by the start of the season. Once practices rolled around, he was given opportunities to prove himself. During one play in practice, the halfback was given the ball on a running play and Matt took a bad angle at him and missed the tackle. The coach started freaking out and told him he didn't think he could play at the college level. To this day, that comment is one of the most defining moments in Matt's life and he was immediately determined to prove his coach wrong. He didn't let a small failure ruin his career; he used it as fuel to motivate him to work harder, showing his initiative in shaping his brand. He adjusted his mindset and routine to dedicate fully to football from that moment on. He would only go out once a week, typically on Saturdays after football games, to enjoy himself and have fun with friends. Aside from that, it was training, studying the playbook more, and playing as hard as possible every time he stepped onto the field. He was determined to prove his coach wrong and that he could not only play at this level, but could excel. By the start of the fall season that year, he worked his way into the starting linebacker position and earned the trust of his coaches.

Throughout his sophomore year, he not only knew what he had to do on every play but also what all of his teammates were supposed to be doing. He was finally himself and all the outside distractions had disappeared. Throughout the whole season, he was very productive on the field and made All Colonial Athletic Association and Walter Camp Football Foundation All American. This was his first break-out season and all of his hard work was finally starting to pay off. That season, the team made it to the semi-finals of the playoffs against Delaware and lost seventeen to three. Although the team fell short of their national championship goals, they had a tremendous season, and so did Matt. The highlight of the season was a game against UMass Amherst at Gillette Stadium. Matt had grown up watching and going to Patriots games as a hometown fan. This was his first opportunity to play on the field he dreamed about growing up. He was excited for this game in particular because UMass had not recruited him coming out of high school. That still stuck with him, and he wanted to prove to them that they made a mistake. In that game, he led UNH with thirteen tackles, forced a fumble, and registered an interception. UNH defeated UMass, and Matt was awarded the Bill Knight Trophy as the game's most valuable player (MVP).

Although he had accomplished a lot that past season, he knew that he could not get complacent. He wanted to continue to be himself and stay true to his personal brand of being the hardest working guy on and off the field. Heading into his junior year, it was his turn to take on leadership responsibilities on the team. On the field, he was already a vocal leader, helping his team on every play. Off the field, he was quiet, humble, and kept to himself. It was the off-the-field leadership that he needed to work on to ensure he was setting a good example. He defined his vision of how he wanted to lead and got to know all the younger players on a personal level and let them know he was there for them. He noticed players who were struggling with the playbook, training, or being homesick and would try to help them the best he could.

During his junior year, he had another outstanding football season. The entire season, he was expected to lead the defense, make the right calls, and make big plays. When the defense was struggling, the coaching staff would look to him to get the team back on track. That junior year season, the team made it to the playoffs and lost to Montana State in the second round by a missed extra point.

Coming off two very productive seasons, people started talking about the possibility of Matt being able to play in the NFL. Although he was humbled by the rumors of going professional, he was the type of person who wasn't going to let outside factors change him. He knew that NFL scouts questioned the play of Division I AA and that his size would continue to be an obstacle for him. However, he stayed hungry to prove he could play at the next level. He was making the most of every opportunity to grow and improve as an athlete. At the end of that season, Matt was acknowledged as the Buck Buchanan Award winner as National Defensive Player of the Year. The award is given annually to the most outstanding defensive player nationally in the Division I Football Championship Subdivision. That same year, he also made All Colonial Athletic Association and Walter Camp Football Foundation All American for the second year in a row.

That spring of 2012, after graduating from UNH with a business degree, Matt started getting multiple calls and visits from NFL agents. However, his focus from the start of pre-season training was on his final season at a school he would forever call home. He wanted to be 100% invested mentally and physically in his last season and ignored any outside distractions. Unfortunately, he did not have as good of a senior season as he had hoped. He didn't make as many plays as he wanted to, and the team lost in the first round of the play-offs. Looking back on the season, Matt was disappointed, but now focused on what was next.

He moved down to Bradenton, Florida for two months that winter to train at the Athletic Edge Sports facility; it was time to prepare for the NFL. During those two months at Athletic Edge Sports, he was getting stretched by a trainer who over-extended and pulled his hamstring. Matt was disappointed as this was a week before the East West Shrine game, the second biggest All-Star game in the country for college prospects. In this game, the nation's top college players are given the opportunity to display their talents to a national television audience and over 300 NFL scouts. Despite the pulled hamstring, he showed up and played through the East West Shrine game. Matt felt that he had actually done pretty well considering his injury, accumulating a few tackles and a fumble recovery. However, he could not just wait and see and continued to move forward.

Next, his focus turned to his pro-day at UNH where he ended up clocking 4.6 seconds in the 40-yard dash despite his nagging hamstring. Afterward, he continued to train and heal in anticipation of the NFL draft. Draft day came and went and he had not received a call. After the draft though, he got invited to rookie mini-camp for both the New England Patriots and the Philadelphia Eagles. Matt was thrilled and grateful to have these opportunities to showcase his abilities.

Growing up watching and rooting for the Patriots as his hometown team, the experience at that rookie mini-camp was a dream come true. Being able to put on the Patriots helmet was a dream realized. After the Patriots mini-camp, Matt went down to the Eagles mini-camp to showcase his skills. Unfortunately, nothing came from either camp, but he was very grateful for both experiences. Looking forward, he felt he was now in limbo and needed to determine what his next steps were going to be.

He was feeling down and went up to UNH to talk to his coach who suggested he look into scouting positions with NFL teams. After that conversation, he started to put things in motion. He contacted every single person he knew and asked for NFL coaching contacts that he could reach out to. Matt knew the competition for scouting positions was stiff and knew he needed to position himself differently to stand out. To do that, he created a project in Microsoft Excel for the 2014 draft class. He had created a database, scouted players, and created formulae that produced a scouting report. Matt sent his project and resume to all of his NFL contacts but nothing worked out. Matt continued to stay dedicated for months and pursued opportunities with the Tampa Bay Buccaneers and New York Jets. Although both teams really liked him, both decided to go in another direction.

Soon enough his persistence paid off when he got an opportunity to interview with the Green Bay Packers for a summer internship. They brought eight prospects in for the interviews, including Matt. He presented to the entire front office and was offered the summer internship position. At the same time, he had also received an opportunity to interview with the Washington Redskins organization for a two-year internship development program. Despite getting the Packers offer, he wanted to do the interview since the program was for two years versus just the summer. After the interview, the Redskins also offered him an internship position.

Matt ended up deciding to take the longer-term opportunity the Redskins offer presented. He moved down to Virginia in July of 2014 to start his internship. His goal going into the internship with the Redskins was to prove his worth, not step on anyone's toes, and showcase both his brand and his passion for football. He started scouting on the professional side and got an opportunity to move over to the college side to broaden his experience. He formed great relationships and the organization was very impressed with his football knowledge, professionalism, and general candor. Through his hard work, he was promoted to a full-time position as a Northeast Area Scout. Matt was given the promotion in under a year, when it typically takes two to three years. This speaks to his work ethic and passion for the game. He was very lucky to find his passion early in life and was not afraid to continue chasing his vision even in the face of adversity.

Matt finished his football career at UNH with 449 tackles, the most in UNH history. His jersey, number 52, was retired at the school in 2013. His vision of himself allowed him to push past obstacles, prove others wrong, and ultimately get others bought into the story he was creating for himself. Today, Matt is in a position where he is truly passionate about his career and has created a story that others want to follow.

If you could go back in time and tell the eighteen-year-old version of yourself one piece of advice for college, what would it be?

Have the confidence to be comfortable in your own skin and know who you are and what your strengths are. No matter what happens to you, what obstacles you have to face, what failures happen along the way, never let it change who you are at your core. Don't waiver, and always continue to stay hungry and go after your goals.

—m—

Sangu Delle
CEO of Golden Palm Investments, Entrepreneur, Author, Clean Water Activist, Soros Fellow, and TEDGlobal Fellow

Like Daquan Oliver and Matt Evans, Sangu Delle is enjoying a career that encompasses a multitude of his talents and interests. If you Google Sangu, you will instantly notice that he is a TED speaker, an entrepreneur, and a philanthropist; in addition, he is currently enrolled in the JD/MBA program at Harvard Law School and Harvard Business School. You will also admire the images of his authentic Ghanaian attire, and notice links to his Twitter and Facebook pages. In a way, Google search results are part of your personal brand. Take a moment to Google yourself. What appears? High school sport stats? Pictures of you from your social media? Hopefully nothing appears that you wish to bury deep in the archives. Now is your time to create what your story will look like for the rest of your life. How will you enhance and augment your Google results and what will searchers deduce about you?

Sangu's public Twitter account has over 2,500 followers and his tweets reflect his commitment to social justice and his entrepreneurial activism. Do you use Twitter? What do your tweets reflect about you?

Transform your social media accounts so they reflect your personal brand and help you connect to people and organizations that will help you grow and discover your interests. You never know what kind of opportunities will come your way when you use your social media accounts to connect with like-minded individuals.

Sangu Delle
November 24 at 3:49pm ·

Friends, looking for female technology entrepreneurs from the following countries. Please DM me if you know someone amazing. Thank you.

Egypt
Morocco
Rwanda
Somalia

Like   Comment   Share

7 people like this.

2 shares

View 1 more comment

Mawuli Dake Rwanda: Denyse Uwineza
Like · Reply · 1 · November 24 at 8:50am

Mawuli Dake Rwanda: Dee Igihawzo
Like · Reply · November 24 at 10:30am

Dee Igihawzo Please feel free to contact Akaliza Keza Gara Hehe Limited
Like · Reply · November 24 at 10:44am

Sangu Delle Thanks so much! I will follow up
Like · Reply · November 27 at 1:22pm

As his Google search results boast, Sangu is an entrepreneur, author, clean water activist, TEDGlobal Fellow, and Soros Fellow. He has been named the Future Award Africa winner for the Young Person of the Year, a *Forbes'* "Top 30 Most Promising Entrepreneurs in Africa," and *Euromoney's* "Africa Rising Star"; all of these accolades speak to his skills in changing the financial, investment, and business landscape in Africa. He is the founder and CEO of Golden Palm Investments (GPI), an investment holding and advisory company focused on developing and growing companies in Africa, as well as the cofounder of Cleanacwa, a nonprofit dedicated to providing water, sanitation, and basic human rights in underdeveloped communities in Ghana. His story is an inspiration to many individuals worldwide and especially to those in Ghana. He credits his upbringing and early experiences, which gave birth to his belief in the power of humility to recognize, learn, and instill change in Africa.

Born with Ghanaian, Egyptian, and Burkinabe roots, Sangu always had a vision of one day attending the prestigious Harvard University and creating an impact in Africa. He was determined to achieve these great heights through hard work and creativity. He always considered himself an entrepreneur. His knack for finding and seizing opportunities manifested as early as he can remember.

Sangu carried this momentum into high school at Ghana International School (GIS). He knew his strengths as an honors student and earned a full-merit scholarship to Peddie School, a reputable college preparatory school in Hightstown, New Jersey. These early experiences were demonstrative of his creativity and entrepreneurial spirit, which continued to progress once he landed in the United States to attend high school. He kept up his elite academic performance at Peddie, graduating Summa Cum Laude, and was the recipient of the Potter Cup, Peddie's highest honor.

His dedication allowed him to achieve his goal of attending Harvard. He faced obstacles during his freshman year while trying to figure out which careers he would be passionate about. As with many college students, he needed to deal with the pressure from his family to pursue a career he was not necessarily passionate about. He was expected to become a doctor because of his intellect, and it was some families' tradition in Africa that the smartest kid aspires to be a doctor.

However, upon arrival at Harvard, he found an interest in economics, finance, policy, and development issues through his studies. At the beginning of his freshman year, he began to reach out to a variety of Harvard alumni by researching and setting up meetings with individuals to talk about their field of work. He recalls asking his mentors to forget about the sexy and glorified job descriptions, and instead he asked the probing questions: "What do you hate about your job? What does your work day look like?" He wanted a real sense of what the careers entailed. Through his efforts, Sangu confirmed his interest in economics and finance.

The next step for him was finding adequate experience in these fields. He chose to pursue an internship in investment banking, aligning his interests to his career. He applied to over ten of the major investment banks and was rejected by every single one of them. Sangu failed forward, thought outside of the box, and decided to go on the Harvard alumni network database to network his way into an internship. The Harvard alumni network database limits you to ninety-nine emails per day and he found this out the hard way. Every single day, he sent out ninety-nine personalized emails to Harvard alumni in hopes of making a connection that would earn him an internship. After three weeks of sending out emails each day, he received a response from his now close friend and mentor from the class of 1987, who was able to get him an internship with Bear Stearns his freshman year.

In addition to his interest in economics and finance, Sangu's childhood interest in impacting Africa remained clear. During his freshman year exploration, he realized that if he wanted to play a role in Africa's development, he needed to be trained not only in business, but in the history of the continent. He endeavored to gain a very rich and comprehensive understanding of the history, culture, and political economy of Africa through a multidisciplinary perspective in subjects such as political science, literature, and public health. In his mind, a combination of economics, finance, and African studies was key for the vision he had of his future to create an impact in Africa.

His motivation to give back to Africa led to the formation of his nonprofit organization called the African Development Initiative (ADI) to create sustainable development projects. For one of his first projects under ADI, Sangu visited a village in Ghana. ADI endeavored to work with the community to provide clean water and sanitation. The initiative designed and implemented Project Access to Clean Water for Agyementi (ACWA) to develop a sustainable water delivery system for a community of 500 in Ghana. This project built momentum for ADI and enabled them to partner with other prominent organizations in Nigeria and Ethiopia. ADI is now formally known as Cleanacwa, and continues to bring clean water and sanitation to hundreds of people across villages in Africa.

During the summer of his sophomore year he interned at Goldman Sachs through their Scholarship for Excellence program. The internship was another piece that fit into his career puzzle and taught him how to think like an investor and to effectively analyze investment opportunities in a variety of industries. Having the urge to create an impact in Africa, and not forgetting his entrepreneurial fire, Sangu was inspired to create what is now known as Golden Palm Investments (GPI).

At a community meeting he had with one of the villages he worked with under Cleanacwa, he asked everyone, "If I had a World Bank budget, and there was a single thing that I could do for you, what would it be?" He thought the majority would ask for money to be shared amongst the people of the village. But to his surprise, the people of the village asked for jobs. They wanted to be economically empowered and it set off a philosophical change in Sangu's mindset. He realized that in order to liberate the African continent, he would have to economically empower people, not just provide handouts and charity aids. He therefore focused his efforts toward figuring out ways GPI could help develop companies in Africa. Beginning in agriculture, he used the knowledge gained from his studies and internships and was able to raise $50,000 in capital as part of his first big deal. He used the capital to import tractors and mechanized a corn farm of over 1,000 acres in Afram Plains in Ghana. The investment was very successful and proceeded to generate jobs in the community, developing GPI's portfolio.[30]

The following summer, he earned an internship with Morgan Stanley. His assignments focused on distress investing, which dealt with companies near or currently going through bankruptcy. It also involved a great deal of legal work, which expanded his breadth of knowledge in that area. This was very helpful in understanding the full landscape of analyzing and making the appropriate investment decisions. He continued to run GPI during this period and was able to leverage both experiences interchangeably to add value to both GPI and Morgan Stanley.

Once he was able to align his passions with the right experiences and opportunities, his next challenge was to convert these interests to a full-time offer. Sangu ended up starting at Morgan Stanley full-time and later found an opportunity to work for Valiant Capital Partners, a hedge fund, where he was involved in all aspects of the investment process, including idea generation, deal sourcing, detailed modeling, and industry research. Over the next two years, he was able to get extensive investing experience, immersed himself in venture capital investing, and looked at deals in Asia, Latin America, Africa, and Europe. After this experience, Sangu felt he had received great foundational training and was now ready to transition the knowledge he acquired to his "baby" - GPI. Throughout his career, he revisited his purpose, passion, and vision on a daily basis to ensure he was showing up in the right way to make his vision a reality.

Today, Sangu runs GPI full time and is pursuing a four-year JD/MBA from Harvard University. GPI now boasts a multimillion dollar valuation and continues to operate in high growth industries funding promising start-ups that can have a social impact and generate jobs in the African economy. GPI has backed start-ups such as SOLO Mobile, a revolutionary new device manufacturing and end-to-end digital content company, and mPharma, a healthcare tech start-up operating in Ghana, Zambia, and Cote D'Ivoire. GPI is currently financing and developing a multimillion-dollar real estate project in the heart of Ghana's capital and continues to focus investments on industries such as healthcare, financial services, and technology, inspiring the growth and social impact Africa deserves.

Sangu does not think he will ever stop dreaming. While running GPI and Cleanacwa full time, he is working on his forthcoming book, *Seeding Growth: Africa's Youngest Entrepreneurs*, scheduled to be published in 2016. He is also curating an angel fund targeting female entrepreneurs in Sub-Saharan Africa. He is motivated by his passion to inspire change and has launched Cleanacwa's 2025 campaign to achieve 100% water and sanitation coverage in Ghana in the next ten years. Sangu's childhood vision may have been blurry, but, over time, he endeavored to make intentional decisions and unlocked the pieces of the career puzzle that not only created his story and developed his brand but also clarified his ultimate vision - to create an impact in Africa - a dream he turned into a reality.

If you could go back in time and tell the eighteen-year-old version of yourself one piece of advice for college, what would it be?

I don't believe in luck, I believe in favor. The most important thing to focus on is the people around you. As much as you are going on your grind, you must make sure you spend your time developing and nurturing relationships with the people [who] matter. Because at the end of the day, that is what matters. Don't be afraid to try new things and make mistakes. Get out of your comfort zone and push the envelope. Always come back at the end of the day, look yourself in the mirror, and ask if you are at peace with yourself balancing your workload, taking good care of yourself, and living a full and happy life.

—⁂—

Creating Your Personal Brand

Communicating your story allows others to understand and buy into your mission. Daquan, Matt, and Sangu each demonstrated how they distinguished themselves in a crowd of many. We cannot emphasize enough that while creating your story is a life-long journey, it is very important to start now. There are many activities out there to help you identify and define your brand to help you start your career in college. Make sure you are taking advantage of them.

(1) **Fast Forward:** Most people are not able to clearly define their vision of their future. However, if you take a few minutes each day to close your eyes, clear your mind, and think about where you want to see yourself, you create an awareness that allows you to make intentional decisions on a daily basis. Visualizing your future while eating breakfast, or in the shower, encourages you to reflect on and make necessary changes in your actions to consistently embody the brand to which you aspire. Remember the amount of focus and discipline it took for Daquan, Matt, and Sangu to stay on track while chasing their careers? It was the vision they had and the hunger to make it a reality that kept them focused.

(2) **Day-to-Day Actions:** Making intentional decisions each day through your actions and interactions with other people gives you greater control over how you are perceived. By visiting your future

each day, you can take actions to align with your brand through the quality of your work product, how you dress, the activities you are involved in, and how you interact with others. You can also set goals for yourself to develop certain skills that you will need to create the future you desire.

(3) **Social Media:** The social media platforms we use, such as Facebook, Instagram, Twitter, and LinkedIn, are the digital versions of ourselves. They extend our personal brand beyond our immediate and visible environment and make it easily accessible to strangers and the world at large. In viewing your social media profiles, you should always ask yourself, *What kind of persona am I showing the public? What does this post suggest about me? Are my interests easily identifiable?* Ensure your personal brand grows and strengthens the right way across all your forums of communication. You can do this by reviewing your social media profiles, posts, and images to make sure there is nothing in conflict with what you perceive your brand to be.

LinkedIn is becoming one of the fastest ways to not only build a network but also to show your resume to the world. As you live out your story through the intentional decisions you make and the different experiences you find yourself in, ensure your LinkedIn profile reflects your current achievements and future aspirations. Use the platform to update your resume, connect with others, post articles of interest to you and your field, and view articles that others are posting to help you understand the trends happening in a specific industry.

(4) **Leadership Opportunities:** Throughout our lives, we are presented with opportunities to be a leader. Whether it's running a team project, being captain of our sports team, or leading a charity food donation drive, leadership experiences allow us to test and shape our personal brand. We can find which aspects of our brand work to inspire others and instill mutual respect. It is a fallacy that some people are leaders and others are followers, everyone has the ability to lead. You don't have to be loud to be a leader. Students should take every leadership opportunity that comes their way and should seek out leadership roles to see which aspects of their brand resonate with others.

(5) **Mirror Those That Inspire You:** Think about the people who inspire you. Which aspects of their brand make you want to emulate them? Think about the positive qualities projected by those around you and

brainstorm how you can incorporate these qualities into your own personal brand.

Ultimately, the power of taking ownership of your career and preparing for your future sets the tone for the type of story you create. Having a strong personal brand communicates confidence which allows you to make meaningful connections and gain more opportunities to test out your interests. The daily decisions you make will put you in a position to build upon your differentiators and develop your story into something that everyone will want to follow.

CHAPTER 5

Managing Your Investment

"Formal education will make you a living; self-
education will make you a fortune."[31]

**JIM ROHN - AMERICAN ENTREPRENEUR,
AUTHOR AND MOTIVATIONAL SPEAKER.**

One of the key aspects of maximizing your return on your college degree is to manage how much you are paying for it. College tuition has increased by over 1,000% since average annual tuition costs started being recorded in 1978.[32] The high cost of college education is the primary reason why so few people in the world actually get the opportunity to go. The most expensive schools in the United States are now upwards of $60,000 per year.[33] Students who are fortunate enough to go to college need to be smart with their finances to ensure they can put their degree to work for them after graduation. The most important aspects of managing your investment in a college degree is to minimize your debt and to create a savings plan that will enable you to kick-start your career upon graduation.

While all college students deal with different financial circumstances, approximately 77% of all students in a four year college or university go full-time.[34] Many of these students are moving out of their parent's house for the first time and are enjoying the personal freedom that college provides. Managing personal finances as a student typically falls to the back of the bus as classes, new friends, activities, and social interactions consume their daily agenda. While college can be an amazing experience and career development opportunity, like any investment – it needs to be managed closely.

Due to the high cost of college education, many students are forced to take out student loans to pay for their tuition. The implications of this debt is not immediately realized by most students because the repayment typically is not required until after graduation. After receiving your degree, you will need to start repaying your student loans which can take up a significant amount of your monthly income. The reason why debt is bad for your financial portfolio is because the government agency, bank, or other financial institution that loaned you the money will charge you interest on your outstanding balance. Interest compensates these institutions for loaning you money and is charged on what is called the "principal" balance, which is simply the amount of money you were loaned plus any accumulated interest. The average college student graduating in 2015 will have to pay back a little more than $30,000 in student loan debt upon graduation. To put that into perspective, $30,000 in student loans at 6% interest would mean that you would be paying approximately $333 dollars a month for ten years after college to pay off the balance. This equates to a total payment of $39,967 and means that you will be paying an additional $9,967 in interest by taking out these loans.[35] The monthly amount may not seem like much, but when it makes up a significant portion of your entry-level salary, you will notice it. The payments put financial pressure on students who typically need to pay for living expenses like rent, utilities, and food. In many cases, students who do not manage their debt levels in college are forced to move back in with their parents or forgo their career aspirations for a stable income.

Take time to understand the differences in the types of student loans you have access to so that you can manage your debt and post-graduation repayment plan. If you need to take out student loans to support your college education payments, you will need to first fill out a Free Application for Federal Student Aid (FAFSA) online. This application is used to determine the amount of federal government grants, loans, and other forms of financial aid available to you.

The FAFSA application allows you to apply for the Federal Direct Loan Program, which is the largest federal student loan program available to students. These loans are the most favorable for students to use and are explained in the chart below.

Type of Federal Direct Loan	Overview
Direct Subsidized (Stafford) Loans	<ul><li>Direct Subsidized Loans are available to undergraduate students with financial need.</li><li>Your school determines the amount you can borrow.</li><li>These are favorable loans for college students to take because the U.S. Department of Education pays the interest on these loans while you're in school at least half-time, and for the first six months after you leave school (referred to as a grace period).</li><li>**Interest rate:** 4.29% (Loans first disbursed on or after 7/1/15 and before 7/1/16)</li></ul>
Direct Unsubsidized (Stafford) Loans	<ul><li>Direct Unsubsidized Loans are available to undergraduate students and there is no requirement to demonstrate financial need.</li><li>Your school determines the amount you can borrow.</li><li>A key difference with unsubsidized loans vs. subsidized is that you are responsible for paying the interest on the outstanding loan balance while in college and during grace periods.</li><li>If you choose not to pay the interest while you are in school and during grace periods, your interest will accumulate and will be added to the principal amount of your loan. This snowball effect can create a much larger loan balance for students to pay off upon graduation.</li><li>**Interest rate:** 4.29% (Loans first disbursed on or after 7/1/15 and before 7/1/16)</li></ul>
Perkins Loans	<ul><li>Loans made through the Federal Perkins Loan Program, often called Perkins Loans, are low-interest federal student loans for undergraduate students with exceptional financial need.</li><li>Only certain schools participate in the Federal Perkins Loan Program so check with your school's financial aid office.</li><li>Your school is the lender; you will make your payments either to the school that disbursed your loan or your school's loan servicer.</li><li>If you are an undergraduate student, you may be eligible to receive up to $5,500 a year.</li><li>**Interest rate:** 5% (Loans first disbursed on or after 7/1/15 and before 7/1/16).</li></ul>
Direct Consolidation Loans	<ul><li>A Direct Consolidation Loan allows you to consolidate (combine) multiple federal education loans into one loan.</li><li>Consolidation loans are typically used to simplify the loan repayment process for students so that they only have to make one monthly payment as opposed to multiple payments on multiple loans.</li></ul>

Source: *https://studentaid.ed.gov/sa/types/loans*

Type of Federal Direct Loan	First-Year Undergraduate Annual Loan Limit	Second-Year Undergraduate Annual Loan Limit	Third-Year and Beyond Undergraduate Annual Loan Limit
Federal Direct Loans	<ul><li>$5,500-$9,500</li><li>No more than $3,500 of this amount may be in subsidized loans.</li></ul>	<ul><li>$6,500-$10,500</li><li>No more than $4,500 of this amount may be in subsidized loans.</li></ul>	<ul><li>$7,500-12,500</li><li>No more than $5,500 of this amount may be in subsidized loans.</li></ul>
	Subsidized and Unsubsidized Aggregate Loan Limit: $31,000—No more than $23,000 of this amount may be in subsidized loans.		
Perkins Loans	If you are an undergraduate student, you may be eligible to receive up to $5,500 a year. The total you can borrow as an undergraduate is $27,500.		

Source: https://studentaid.ed.gov/sa/types/loans

For students who need to take out more loans than what is available through the Federal Direct Loan and Perkins Loan Programs, private loans are available through banks and other financial institutions. One of the most important aspects of shopping for the best private student loans is to realize they have variable interest rates. Federal loans carry a fixed interest rate meaning that the interest rate will not change over the life of the loan. Variable interest rates fluctuate throughout the year based on the rate banks pay each other to borrow money. There is no legal limit on the interest rate private lenders can charge you, but typical private student loans charge 12% interest. That is almost three times the interest that federal loans charge, so you want to do your homework before taking out a private loan. Similar to federal unsubsidized loans, private loans start charging interest right when the loan is granted which can greatly increase the loan balance upon graduation. Make sure you shop the market for the private loans with the lowest interest rate and best terms. Students should exhaust all of their federal loan options before taking out a private loan.

One way to minimize the amount of debt students need to take on to pay for college is to be awarded a scholarship or grant. The financial aid letter you receive from your school will detail the estimated cost of attending that college, as well as the total for scholarships, grants, and loans – and what you need to pay out of pocket. According to a study from NerdScholar, around $2.9 billion dollars of federal grant money was left unclaimed in 2014 after high school seniors neglected to complete the Free Application for Federal Status Aid.[36] The key difference between grants and scholarships is that grants are based on financial need and scholarships are based on merit (i.e., being an outstanding student). There are a number of options available; the key is to research what those options are. Christopher Gray won $1.3 million in scholarships through hard work, grit, and determination which paid for his entire college tuition, room, and board. To help other students, he founded Scholly which was featured on SharkTank and connects students and families with the best scholarship matches for their situation. Putting in the work upfront to get any and all grants and scholarships that you can will pay off when you graduate with less (or no) debt.

For students who are not working while in college, it is also easy to get in other forms of debt by over using credit cards and consumer loans. Banks and other financial institutions have been marketing credit cards to students for years. The problem with credit products is that it is very easy to purchase things even when we do not have cash readily available. Credit cards require you to pay the outstanding balance on a monthly basis, or at least some portion of it. Any unpaid balance each month will be charged interest which is on average 19.80% on student credit cards.[37] Credit cards have some of the highest interest rates among credit products offered by banks and other financial institutions. For instance, if you didn't pay your $100 monthly credit card balance, you would be charged $19.80 in interest. If students keep a large outstanding balance on their credit cards, the principal balance of the loan will begin to multiply due to a term called compound interest. In this example, if you missed your payment during two statement periods, the interest in the second period would be charged on $119.80. Instead of $19.80 in interest, you will be charged $23.72 (19.80% of $119.80) which will increase your total loan balance to $143.52. As you can see, this is why debt can grow to become unmanageable, if not closely monitored and paid down.

Another way to minimize your debt upon graduation is to work while you are in school. Many colleges offer programs for students to earn money on campus. These employment opportunities range from being an RA of a dorm, working for the school's accounts payable department, or soliciting donations from alumni. Inquire about what opportunities are available for you. Earning money while in college is not only good practical work experience, but some of this money can be put aside to pay for part of your college education. Learning to save money is an important principle of personal finance. By saving at least 10-20% of each paycheck you earn, you will be able to pay for some of your tuition or books down the line to minimize the amount you need to pay via student loans. It is important to note that some students go to college part-time while working to support themselves or a family on top of their education bills. Being smart with your finances, regardless of your situation, allows you to graduate college with good financial standing– ready to conquer your dreams.

Paid internships, part-time jobs, and apprenticeships are the best ways to get hands on practical experience and earn a good paycheck. Depending on your field of study, the overall pay can range but you will be earning a consistent paycheck for either a semester or a summer. Knowing how much you will be making every week allows you to budget and figure out how much you can save over the entire period. Budgets are a quick way to analyze your income vs. your expenses to see what your overall cash flow is (your money coming in and out). Track how much you spend on food, going out, and other expenses for a week and see where you can potentially cut down to minimize your overall expenses. There are great online tools like Mint that allow you to sync up all your bank accounts, credit cards, and other financial accounts to show an overall view of your personal finances. These tools can help you flag areas where you might be overspending. In turn, you can create a savings plan that will help you improve your financial position.

An additional way to earn income in college is through competitions and challenges. Depending on your field of study, competitions and challenges vary but can include: innovation, social impact, case study, entrepreneurship, health care, writing, debate, finance, and hackathons. These competitions are meant to bring out the best in students and challenge them to make an impact. Tara won the Goldman Sachs Trading Competition, Remy won the Entrepreneurship Competition at Suffolk University, and John Harthorne won the MIT Entrepreneurship Competition for $100,000. Ask your career service department for information on competitions or challenges hosted through your college or other organizations. You should also look online for student competitions or challenges related to your field of study. In some cases, these competitions and challenges pay out scholarships instead of cash prizes, but you can use those scholarships to pay for tuition and minimize your overall student debt.

Once you graduate, there are many upfront costs when getting out on your feet. If you are renting a place to live close to your new job, you should be prepared to pay first and last month's rent in full upon signing the lease. Renting also comes with paying bills such as electric, heat, hot water, internet, cable, and renters insurance. You may also have a commuting expense, need to buy new clothes for work, or have other job related expenses. Some college-grads even have to move around the world to start their new job which can be expensive. The point is, the more money you have in your savings account to support these upfront expenses upon graduation, the easier it is to transition into adulthood. It starts by planning ahead each year of college to find new opportunities to earn income while taking classes. You can be creative with your time and find ways to still have fun in college while also earning income and getting relevant job experience.

For the vast majority of college students who graduate and work for a company, organization, or government agency, the employer will offer an employee benefits package which offers 401(k) (retirement plan), health insurance, life insurance, dental insurance, vision insurance, and other supplemental benefits. For instance, if you contribute 10% of each paycheck to your 401(k) for retirement, some employers will match a percentage of that contribution. Setting aside an extra 10% from your paycheck will not impact your weekly life, but over time with compounding interest, you will be better off in the future. Some companies will even support your gym membership or help pay for advanced learning. These details will typically be highlighted in your offer letter. Employee benefits maximize your return on a college degree by providing you with additional financial incentives you otherwise would have to pay for.

Going to college can be a liberating experience, but what feels even better is when you graduate knowing that you have a degree and are ready to start your career in a good financial position. Managing your investment in college and thinking ahead will help to ensure your degree is worth something upon graduation. If you have a great degree and found a career you are passionate about pursuing but cannot because of debt repayment obligations, then what was the point of going to college? Stay on top of your debt, take advantage of every opportunity for grants and scholarships, and find ways to earn some income in college to keep good financial footing. Don't be thinking about college ten or twenty years after you have graduated because you still have to pay your monthly student loan bills.

CHAPTER 6

Press Fast Forward

"Life is about making an impact, not making an income."[38]

- KEVIN KRUSE - *NY TIMES* BEST SELLING AUTHOR

Thinking about where you want to be when you graduate seems like a daunting task if you ask most students entering college. There seems to be an endless amount of time to "figure it out." Remember how fast high school went by? College will go by even faster, so it is important that you are maximizing your return on investment starting from freshman year. All of the individuals that we interviewed for *Fast Forward* didn't get to where they are today without making the conscientious effort to step out of their comfort zone, take risks, and make sacrifices. They made intentional decisions to drive their careers and today are not only a success in their industries doing what they enjoy, but they are also positively impacting society. Being able to wake up each day knowing you are making an impact doing something you love is priceless compared to the majority of people who just "go to work." By 2025, millennials will represent 75% of the global workforce.[39] Millennials and Generation Z will be the most educated generations in history.[40] With that knowledge, we have the power to make a bigger impact on the world than any other generation before us. Don't settle for just a paycheck, create your own path and find a career that you can be proud of.

The concepts laid out in this book are your framework for maximizing what your college degree will be worth. Drawing on a blank sheet of paper to experience different careers first hand, making new connections, and creating your story will increase your odds of finding a career you are passionate about. The young leaders across the world exercise these concepts simultaneously on a daily basis to make their visions a reality. They cannot be done in isolation; each one supports and complements the other. Additionally, managing your personal finances ensures you have the financial capacity and mindset to pursue the career that excites you after graduation.

Start putting these concepts into action to find careers you actually enjoy and maximize the return on your investment in college. Leverage the resources available to you that were noted in each chapter to get started. To recap, here is a short summary of each concept.

(1) **Drawing on a blank sheet of paper:**

In order to find out what you are passionate about, make an effort to experience new things firsthand. It is not enough to just think about your interests and hope you are on the right track. College is one of the most opportune times to experience as much as possible and learn from failures along the way. Life is not laid out on a syllabus; find your passions through experimentation, brainstorm on that blank sheet of paper, make those ideas happen, and pursue careers that motivate you outside of the classroom.

(2) **Making connections:**

Networking may sound evil and one sided, but connecting is mutual, necessary, and what we humans as social beings are all about. Real connections with people built on a foundation of trust and similar sets of values will not only open new doors but also awaken new ideas and interests you never knew you had. Reevaluate your current network regularly to ensure it's up to date and if changes need to be made. Lastly, take the time to meet new and diverse people who can challenge your perceptions of the world and who can open up doors for you that you never thought were possible.

(3) Creating your story:

We all carry different identities at different points in our lives based on our experiences and circumstances. Once you have zeroed in on your career interests and know what you are driving toward, use that knowledge to shape your personal brand to create a cohesive and compelling story. How you show up each and every day and interact with others greatly affects external perceptions of you. Understanding your values, your goals, and your strengths will allow you to create your own story that others will want to follow.

(4) Managing Your Investment:

Make smart decisions to minimize your debt upon graduation. Take advantage of grants and scholarships and find ways to earn income in college each semester to help pay for tuition, books, and other expenses. Create a savings plan and save 10-20% of each paycheck earned to ensure you will be in good financial position once you graduate. Building good personal financial planning habits in college will pay dividends for the rest of your life.

Stephanie Weiner, Amy Robinson, John Harthorne, Karen Kaplan, Daniel Koh, Tara Chang, Katrina Melesciuc, Remy Carpinito, Daquan Oliver, Matt Evans, and Sangu Delle all have different stories with common themes. Each one had to overcome obstacles and setbacks along the path to personal success. They approached these challenges as learning experiences and each had a deep belief in their own abilities. They all made connections along the way that helped support their missions, and created personal brands that made them stand out from their peers. Now consider the fact that they are only eleven individuals from the northeast region of the United States. Imagine how many other people in this world are out there following their passions, taking chances, and making an impact on the world. Anyone with the drive and will to put in the work can create the future they envision.

As the young leaders of today, we owe it to ourselves to create massive value and change the status quo. Let's be innovative and disruptive to create positive change for our communities and for the world. Those who are following their passions are disruptive and do not follow the norms of society. They create their own path forward to achieving their goals and aspirations. Take responsibility for your future outside of the classroom and create a story that you will be proud to look back on.

Fast Forward was written for you. We want to inspire college students to become the young leaders that the future needs to prosper. Our generation faces many challenges such as climate change, population growth, and food and water scarcity. At the same time, technological innovation is changing our lives at a constantly growing pace. Think about how much Facebook, Apple, Google, and Uber have changed people's daily lives. These companies would not have been here today without people who were willing to dream big, take a risk, trust in their network, and try something different.

As college students, you are each in a rich position with tools, professors, clubs, and the brand of your college backing you to help make your dream a reality. Now it's up to you to make the most of them. Will you use all that's been given to you to fast forward to the next step?

Once you start your professional career after graduation, you can apply these same concepts to stay ahead of your peers. We hope this book has inspired you to start thinking about your future and how to use your time in college to be a launchpad for the rest of your life. Take ownership of your future, fail forward, and create your story that will inspire others.

Start your career today, and write what comes next...

The Infamous Resume And Cover Letter

I n the world we live in today, resumes and cover letters are still basic requirements of any job application. Resumes and cover letters are your ticket to
getting the interview. People spend a significant amount of time and effort
thinking about and writing their resumes and tailoring their cover letters for
the position they are applying to. This is the one part of the internship or job
offer process you can actually control. It presents an opportunity for you to
stand out and for potential employers to get to know who you are. Below we
have listed some simple things you can do to ensure your resume and cover
letter not only stand out but speak about who you are, what you are interested
in, and where you want to go.

Enhancing Your Resume:

(1) **Show The Impact:** An employer generally has about fifteen to thirty
seconds to read your resume and make a decision on whether to bring
you in for an interview. A great way to differentiate yourself on paper
is to showcase the impact you made in your relevant career experiences. This is your chance to turn your activities into accomplishments and to show your potential employers what you are capable of.
Having the ability to tell your story on paper is what will transcend to
the reader. Think about the profound stories or articles that grab your
attention. There is almost always a number or statistic or percentage

that peaks your interest. This is the same concept you should take with sharing your experiences. What are the activities you did and how were the people, company or organization affected by what you did? The answers to this question are called impact statements. For example, "Created a sales pipeline database in excel for over fifty clients that enabled our sales representatives to target new opportunities and increase sales by 20%," is an impact statement that answers the three one-word questions you must answer for every accomplishment you state: what, why, and how. All impact statements should start with strong verbs such as developed, created, established, etc. to demonstrate the weight of your accomplishments. Employers are less interested in the specific activities you have done and more interested in what the impact or outcome was.

(2) **The One Page Rule:** The amount of emphasis put on resumes can cause students to over think them. It is best practice to keep your resume to one page. Make sure to use the familiar fonts such as Georgia and Times New Roman as well as keep the font size between nine and twelve. When highlighting your relevant experiences, start with the most recent one and remember to mention the complete name of the company or organization, what they do, and how long you were there for. Lastly, proofread, proofread, and proofread! Even ask friends and family to read over your resume for you. Your resume is the first impression your potential employer has of you so you want to make sure it is of the highest quality and looks professionally formatted.

(3) **Work Backwards:** Most students often make a common mistake in thinking that they do not have adequate experience for the position they are applying for. You must remember that relevant experience is the right experience. Read the job requirements and think of experiences or activities from your past that are relevant. You can use these experiences to frame your resume so that it appears to align with the requirements of the job. For instance, if the job requires strong data skills, think of instances in your past either within or outside of class where you have had to analyze a lot of data. You want to frame your resume so that you are striking the right cords with the recruiter so that they want to bring you in to learn more about you via an interview.

Making Your Cover Letter Stand Out:

(1) **Make It Pop:** Similar to an employer only having about fifteen to thirty seconds to review your resume, the same can be said for your cover letter. Try to keep your cover letter to one page. Make sure to use short and active sentences to engage the reader. You could even break out some key points of the cover letter into bullet points to make the statements stand out. An example of what could be listed out as bullets are your skills and accomplishments from a specific experience. A simple, easy to read cover letter is more attractive than a cover letter with wordy paragraphs and complex sentence structures. Upon first glance, the employer is also likely to make a decision based off the first paragraph of your cover letter. Ensure this paragraph grabs the attention of your potential employer to entice him or her to keep reading. One way of doing this within the paragraph is to be bold and express the reasons why you are the right candidate for the position you are applying for.

(2) **Explain Your Why:** If you do not know why you are applying for the position, you are probably applying for the wrong one and more than likely will not get the offer. You should always have a reason why you are applying for a position at a company and that should be expressed in your cover letter. This answers the "Why should I even hire him or her?" question that every employer will ask themselves when recruiting for an opening within their company. Your resume and cover letter are known to complement each other. Think of your cover letter as the document that tells the employer why they should read your resume.

(3) **Make It Personal:** Your cover letter is your opportunity to build a relationship with your potential employer. Try to find out who to directly address the cover letter to. It makes your letter more personal, and will increase the likelihood of it being read in the first place. The ability to sell your background and experiences by showcasing the impact you created and are capable of allows the reader to envision possibilities for the company once you are on board. Great cover letters usually have one or two stories illustrating your possession of the

skills that are required to get the job done. Remember the three one-word questions you must answer for every accomplishment on your resume: what, why, and how? Use the same formula when articulating each story in your cover letter to demonstrate the impact you have made. People generally relate to stories, and everyone wants to hear a good story. Once you are able to tell your unique story on your cover letter, you will be one step closer to getting called in for an interview.

Your resume and cover letter are your first impressions to the organization you want to work for. Allow your story to resonate through your experiences and let the words you write speak for themselves.

BONUS CHAPTER

How To Ace
The Interview

Interviews are a part of every internship and job offer process. Although, interviews may seem daunting, we are going to outline three easy tips to start thinking differently about the process to maximize your likelihood of getting the position you want. As mentioned earlier in the book, the global competition for internship or entry level job opportunities is only increasing as college continues to become a minimum requirement for top employers. Find ways to stand out, convey your personal brand, and stand out as the best candidate for the job.

(1) **Do Your Homework:** When preparing for any interview, the first step is to be very well researched on the organization including what their purpose is, what they do, and who they serve. Understand the roles, responsibilities and qualifications of the specific position you are trying to obtain. Print the internship or job application and next to each listed role or responsibility, try to write an example of how you have demonstrated that in the past. The best place to start the majority of your research is on the organization's website and other online career platforms like Glassdoor and LinkedIn. These online platforms will provide insight into the organization as well as how they are perceived by current or prior employees. Through your research, create a one page word document of key findings and areas of interest. Know enough about the company where you feel confident carrying a conversation about it if asked. Another great pre-interview activity is to research your interviewers, and write down one or two

things about them and their career that you can draw on in the interview. Ultimately, the amount of preparation you put in will increase your confidence and will reflect how much you want the position versus your peers.

(2) **Change Your Mindset:** Think about interviewing as not only the company figuring out whether you are a good fit for them, but also if the company and position are the right fit for you. If you take this approach, interviews become a lot less scary. Use this mindset as an opportunity to conduct your own interview; uncover the responses to the questions you were not able to find during your research. The interviewers will be intrigued that you are prepared and generally interested in learning more about the company. Ask your interviewer about their path within the company. People love to talk about their stories and their accomplishments. As they describe their career path, use it as an opportunity to ask more questions around certain aspects of the company they uncover. Getting the conversation flowing in an interview is your job, not the interviewers.

(3) **Come Prepared:** It's game time, and the best way to ensure you stand out is to come prepared. Research the company's dress code that you are interviewing for – mirror that style, if not sure, the defacto rule of thumb is to dress formally. Men should preferably wear a suit and tie and women should wear a formal dress or suit. Wear minimal jewelry, a neat hairstyle, and be professional. First impressions make a huge impact. Come prepared with several copies of your resume and a business card with your contact information. Websites like Vistaprint are available for students to create cheap and professional business cards for interviews that display their personal brand. In addition, prepare a list of your top five questions from your research. These should be questions about the company or position that intrigued you to want to learn more. Having these questions on you during the interview is a great way to start the conversation and show that you did your homework. In order to ensure you stand out, think about not only your words, but your body language. Are you slouching? Are you rigid? Do you cross your arms? Do you play with your hair? If you are not sure, perhaps you can try a mock interview with someone

in career services or a professor. Choose someone older rather than a close friend to mock interview you. They'll notice things that a peer might not. Finally, even if you have a strong connection with your interviewer, it's important to stay professional.

In many cases, you are not competing against the other interviewees but more so yourself. Control your emotions and stay confident in your capabilities by putting in the work well in advance to ensure you stand out.

Tucker Matheson & Pichon Duplan

Tucker Matheson and Pichon Duplan have worked together for several years at a professional services firm doing management consulting. Their friendship grew with a common goal to help students navigate college and start their careers.

—⁓—

Tucker grew up twenty minutes south of Boston, Massachusetts. Outside of management consulting, Tucker previously taught personal financial planning for three years as an adjunct professor at his alma mater, Suffolk University, and is now a member of Suffolk's Young Alumni Advisory Board. Tucker was nominated in 2015 to be one of four staff in the United States to lead his company's Advisory National Staff Council, providing recommendations on pressing topics and company initiatives to his company's senior leadership team. His experience teaching and coaching students and his leadership roles within the company he works for inspired his eagerness to give back and help other college students jump-start their careers. In his spare time, Tucker enjoys traveling, working out, constantly learning, eating good food, and spending time with family and friends.

—⚭—

Pichon, born in Los Angeles but raised in Ghana, has been making an impact outside of his career in management consulting. While attending Babson College, he cofounded a nonprofit organization called iStandAbove (iSA). The nonprofit equips students with leadership tools and resources to become the best version of themselves. In 2012, Pichon was nominated to serve on his company's National Staff Council and two years later, to lead the Northeast Staff Advisory Council, working with senior leadership to create a true and unique development experience for the company's staff. Soon after, he was elected to serve on the  Advisory Board of the Managing Partner for his company's Northeast Market to provide his perspective and potential solutions to business and diversity and inclusion issues and topics. In his spare time, Pichon loves spending time with family and friends, working out, learning different ways to develop both himself and others, and enjoying a good meal.

—⚭—

Tucker and Pichon's college and professional journey allowed them to have diverse experiences and test out their interests. Along the way, they made great connections that helped catapult them forward in both their careers and personal lives. In their late twenties, Tucker and Pichon have not yet realized the full vision they have for their careers; however, both have been lucky to have started the journey early on. They have learned from their failures and continuously seek opportunities to grow and develop into the best versions of themselves.

If you could go back in time and tell the eighteen-year-old version of yourself one piece of advice for college, what would it be?

Tucker: Through continued hard work and personal achievement, you build up confidence in your skills to tackle bigger goals. Eventually you get to a point where you have a true sense of who you are as an individual (your personal brand), what you are capable of, and what impact you are trying to make on the world. Getting to that point in your life takes time, but it is one of the most rewarding feelings you will ever have. To make it happen, take risks, make new connections, and start pushing the envelope of what you think is possible. I truly believe that anyone can do anything they set their mind to in today's world. We may all be starting from a different place with different resources, but anything is possible if you have the confidence, determination, and work ethic to make it happen. There are no handouts in this world; make your own future happen and do not be afraid to fail forward. Be the hardest worker in the room and create your own story, because no one can get you to where you want to go faster than you can.

Pichon: "Anything worth having in this world never comes easy." My mom spoke these words of wisdom to my brother and me when we were younger. To most, difficult situations are seen as an obstacle. However, it should present nothing but an opportunity to challenge yourself and continue to grow and potentially learn something new. You should always be obsessed with improving as an individual each and every day. Having this obsession gives you a clear vision of how you can make intentional and impactful decisions in your life—decisions that will lead you toward your version of success. With this mindset, no matter the situation, you will ask the right questions, make the right decisions and surround yourself with the right people to make the impossible seem like a natural occurrence.

Help Us Spread The Word

D id you enjoy reading *Fast Forward*? Please take a moment to write a review for us on Amazon. Reviews help other college students find us and maximize the impact this book can have.

Want to stay connected? Visit us at www.pressff.com to see what else we are up to. Subscribe to our YouTube channel where we spotlight different careers and trends. Share a link to one of our videos or our website to help us spread the word to other young leaders.

Use #pressfastforward on Instagram to share your career journey with us and have the chance to be spotlighted on our page.

Acknowledgments

Writing this book has been a tremendously rewarding experience both personally and professionally. Our hope is that *Fast Forward* will inspire college students to start leveraging the framework and tools outlined to maximize their time and investment in college. There is no time like the present to make intentional steps to find careers that both motivate and excite you.

Although we had the support of each other as co-authors, we also had the support of many other individuals throughout the process. First we would like to thank the people who made the book itself possible; our interviewees: Stephanie Weiner, Amy Robinson, John Harthorne, Karen Kaplan, Daniel Koh, Tara Chang, Katrina Melesciuc, Remy Carpinito, Daquan Oliver, Matt Evans, and Sangu Delle. Our sincere appreciation also goes out to our editors Petrina Pappas and Matthew Bobryk who were instrumental in the development of this book. We would also like to thank all those we collaborated with for feedback, guidance, and support: Margaret Burke, Stacy Cutchall, John Sviokla, Michael Fenlon, J.C. Lapierre, Susan Brennan, Elizabeth Ziegler, Dasha Maximov, Stephanie Nearhos, and Nish Acharya.

We would also like to say a BIG thank you to our family and friends for always being there, believing in us, and for giving us the platform to continue reaching for our highest potential. Without you, none of this would be possible.

Lastly, our greatest gratitude goes out to all our readers. You rock! Remember, you will make or break the mission of this book. Stay committed to your vision and own your future. Thank you for reading *Fast Forward* and we hope you will inspire another student to start maximizing their time in college. Help us spread the word and stay in touch! We want to hear from you and about your career journey, please visit us at www.pressff.com.

Many thanks!

Tucker and Pichon

Index

Notes

Preface: The Fast Forward Story
[1] Dave Kerpen, "The 2 Most Important Days In Your Life," Inc., July 8, 2013, http://www.inc.com/dave-kerpen/leadership-the-most-important-days-in-your-life.html

Chapter 1: Maximizing Your Return On Investment
[2] Kofi Annan, "Secretary-General Kofi Annan's opening address to the fifty-third annual DPI/NGO Conference," *United Nations,* August 29, 2000, accessed January 17, 2016, http://www.un.org/dpi/ngosection/annualconfs/53/sg-address.html

[3] Anthony Carnevale, Stephen Rose and Ban Cheah, "The College Payoff," The Georgetown University Center on Education and the Workforce, https://cew.georgetown.edu/wp-content/uploads/2014/11/collegepayoff-complete.pdf

[4] "College Enrollment and Work Activity of 2014 High School Graduates," U.S. Bureau of Labor Statistics, last modified May 19, 2015, accessed January 17, 2016, http://www.bls.gov/news.release/hsgec.nr0.htm

[5] Geoff Maslen, "Worldwide student numbers forecast to double by 2025," *University World News* (London, UK), February 19, 2012, http://www.universityworldnews.com/article.php?story=20120216105739999

[6] "Defining Globalization," *GPF Global Policy Forum,* accessed January 17, 2016, https://www.globalpolicy.org/globalization/defining-globalization.html

[7] "Defining Globalization," *GPF*.

[8] Dylan Love, "Steve Job's 13 Most Inspiring Quotes," *Inc.*, April 15, 2013, http://www.inc.com/dylan-love/steve-jobs-most-inspiring-quotes.html?cid=readmore

Chapter 2: Drawing on a Blank Sheet of Paper

[9] Adam Bryant, "Stewart Butterfield of Slack: Is Empathy on Your Résumé?" *The New York Times*, July 11, 2015, http://www.nytimes.com/2015/07/12/business/stewart-butterfield-of-slack-experience-with-empathy-required.html?_r=0

[10] Herminia Ibarra, *Working Identity: Unconventional Strategies for Reinventing Your Career* (Boston: Harvard Business School Press, 2014), 31.

[11] Ibarra, *Working Identity*, 75.

[12] Ibarra, *Working Identity*, 85.

[13] http://www.forbes.com/pictures/fhgl45hjeg/stephanie-weiner-22/

[14] James Brightman, "Mobile gaming installed base tops 1 billion–IDC," *Games Industry* (Brighton, UK), December 11, 2014, http://www.gamesindustry.biz/articles/2014-12-11-mobile-gaming-installed-base-tops-1-billion-idc

[15] Figures referenced above are as of April 2015.

[16] Figures referenced above are as of April 2015.

Chapter 3: Making Connections

[17] Kevin Kruse, "Stephen Covey: 10 Quotes That Can Change Your Life," *Forbes*, July 16, 2012, http://www.forbes.com/sites/kevinkruse/2012/07/16/the-7-habits/

[18] Ibarra, *Working Identity*, 60.

[19] Melissa Giovagnoli and Jocelyn Carter-Miller, *Networlding: Building Relationships and Opportunities for Success* (San Francisco: Jossey-Bass, 2014), 17.

[20] Giovagnoli and Carter-Miller, *Networlding*, 19.

[21] Giovagnoli and Carter-Miller, *Networlding*, 6.

[22] Giovagnoli and Carter-Miller, *Networlding*, 28.

[23] Giovagnoli and Carter-Miller, *Networlding*, 9.

[24] Giovagnoli and Carter-Miller, *Networlding*, 113.

[25] Giovagnoli and Carter-Miller, *Networlding*, 51.

[26] Hilary Sargent, "This is the most powerful 30-year-old in Boston," *Boston Globe*, December 8, 2015, http://www.boston.com/news/local/massachusetts/2015/12/08/this-the-most-powerful-year-old-boston/1ElaFPlUS6bm6JIy0OReAL/story.html

Chapter 4: Creating Your Story

[27] John Purkiss, "How to build your personal brand," *The Guardian*, September 25, 2012, http://www.theguardian.com/careers/build-personal-brand
[28] Geoff Maslen, "Worldwide student numbers forecast to double by 2025," *University World News* (London, UK), February 19, 2012, http://www.universityworldnews.com/article.php?story=20120216105739999
[29] Glenn Llopis, "Personal Branding Is A Leadership Requirement, Not a Self-Promotion Campaign," *Forbes*, April 8, 2013, http://www.forbes.com/sites/glennllopis/2013/04/08/personal-branding-is-a-leadership-requirement-not-a-self-promotion-campaign

Chapter 5: Managing Your Investment

[30] "Harvard Graduate Sangu Delle of Golden Palm Investments on Ndani TV's Young CEO" BellaNaija.com, July 7, 2014, https://www.bellanaija.com/2014/07/harvard-graduate-sangu-delle-of-golden-palm-investments-on-ndani-tvs-young-ceo-watch/
[31] Rob Berger, "Top 100 Money Quotes of All Time," *Forbes*, April 30, 2014, http://www.forbes.com/sites/robertberger/2014/04/30/top-100-money-quotes-of-all-time/#6cfbee2c675e
[32] Michelle Jamrisko and Ilan Kotlet, "Cost of College Degree in US Soars 12Fold," Bloomberg, August 15, 2012, http://www.bloomberg.com/news/articles/2012-08-15/cost-of-college-degree-in-u-s-soars-12-fold-chart-of-the-day
[33] Troy Onink, "Use These 8 Loans to Pay for College," Forbes, January, 22, 2013, http://www.forbes.com/sites/troyonink/2013/01/22/use-these-8-loans-to-pay-for-college/#3da266fd3dd1
[34] "Characteristics of Postsecondary Students," National Center for Education Statistics, May 2015, http://nces.ed.gov/programs/coe/indicator_csb.asp
[35] Stephen Dash, "How Much Will You Actually Pay for $30K in Student Loans?" The Huffington Post, May 5, 2016, http://www.huffingtonpost.com/stephen-dash/how-much-will-you-actuall_b_7214518.html

[36] Medha Imam, "$2.9 billion unused federal grant awards in last academic year," USAToday College, January 20, 2015, http://college.usatoday.com/2015/01/20/2-9-billion-unused-federal-grant-awards-in-last-academic-year/

[37] Jonathan Wu, "Average Credit Card Interest Rates (APR) - 2016," ValuePenguin, http://www.valuepenguin.com/average-credit-card-interest-rates

Chapter 6: Press Fast Forward

[38] Kevin Kruse, "Top 100 Inspirational Quotes," *Forbes*, May 28, 2013, http://www.forbes.com/sites/kevinkruse/2013/05/28/inspirational-quotes/

[39] Dan Schawbel, "Why You Can't Ignore Millennials," *Forbes*, September 4, 2013, http://www.forbes.com/sites/danschawbel/2013/09/04/why-you-cant-ignore-millennials/

[40] The Council of Economic Advisors, "15 Economic Facts About Millennials," October 2014, accessed January 17, 2016, https://www.whitehouse.gov/sites/default/files/docs/millennials_report.pdf